Teaching Leadership

American University Studies

Series XIV
Education

Vol. 40

PETER LANG
New York • Washington, D.C./Baltimore
Bern • Frankfurt am Main • Berlin • Vienna • Paris

Teaching Leadership

Essays in Theory and Practice

Edited by
Peter S. Temes

PETER LANG
New York • Washington, D.C./Baltimore
Bern • Frankfurt am Main • Berlin • Vienna • Paris

Library of Congress Cataloging-in-Publication Data

Teaching leadership: essays in theory and practice/ [edited by] Peter S. Temes.
p. cm. —(American university studies. Series XIV, Education; v. 40)
Includes bibliographical references.
1. Leadership—Study and teaching. I. Temes, Peter S. II. Series.
HM141.T39   303.3'4'09711—dc20   95-34823
ISBN 0-8204-2862-0
ISSN 0740-4565

Die Deutsche Bibliothek-CIP-Einheitsaufnahme

Teaching leadership: essays in theory and practice/
Peter S. Temes (ed.). – New York; Washington, D.C./Baltimore; Bern;
Frankfurt am Main; Berlin; Vienna; Paris: Lang.
(American university studies. Ser. 14, Education; Vol. 40)
ISBN 0-8204-2862-0
NE: Temes, Peter S. [Hrsg]; American university studies/ 14

Photograph on the front cover by Taylor A. Lawrence.
Cover design by Nona Reuter.

The paper in this book meets the guidelines for permanence and durability
of the Committee on Production Guidelines for Book Longevity
of the Council of Library Resources.

© 1996 Peter Lang Publishing, Inc., New York

All rights reserved.
Reprint or reproduction, even partially, in all forms such as microfilm,
xerography, microfiche, microcard, and offset strictly prohibited.

Printed in the United States of America.

Table of Contents

Acknowledgments — vii

Introduction — ix
Peter S. Temes

1 Can Leadership Be Studied? — 1
Jacob Heilbrunn

2 Antipodes: Plato, Nietzsche, and the Moral Dimension of Leadership — 13
Paul F. Johnson

3 "Leadership Studies": A Critical Appraisal — 45
Daniel Born

4 Teaching Leadership/Teaching Ethics: Martin Luther King's "Letter From Birmingham Jail" — 73
Peter S. Temes

5 Plato's *Republic* as Leadership Text — 83
Paul F. Johnson

6 Understanding Destructive Obedience: The Milgram Experiments — 105
Mark E. Sibicky

7 Earl Warren, Thurgood Marshall, *Brown v. Board of Education of Topeka*: Portraits in Leadership — 127
Thomas D. Cavenagh

8	Reflections on Gender, Work, and Leadership *Judith Lorber*	147
9	Mujaheddin and Militiamen: The Global Challenge of Esoteric Leadership *Garth Katner*	163
10	Ethics, Chaos, and the Demand for Good Leaders *Joanne Ciulla*	181

Acknowledgments

Jacob Heilbrunn's essay is reprinted by permission of *Wilson Quarterly*.

Judith Lorber's essay is reprinted by permission of Yale University Press.

Gratitude is extended to both, and to all our authors, for permission to publish their work in this volume.

Introduction

This book began with a group of young scholars who found each other lurking in the back rooms and corridors of conferences devoted to the study of leadership. We shared a sense of opportunities being missed. So much of the talk at the conferences was about the most superficial, least challenging aspects of leadership.

Serious scholarship should be more rigorous, should speak to the classic texts of our academic disciplines, and should not tread so lightly around the more troubling aspects of leadership.

In January of 1995, I invited most of the contributors of this volume to a small gathering at Harvard University, where we compared notes and spent long hours confirming our suspicions that the study of leadership could indeed be more exciting and more substantial than the fare we had encountered.

And so we decided to prepare this book. Joanne Ciulla, a name to reckon with in leadership studies, agreed to write an essay in response to the other contributions in this volume, and she deserves great thanks for that effort. Don Bigelow of the U.S. Department of Education attended our January meeting and served as a prod and critical chorus, giving us all an important sense of audience as we proceeded. Benjamin DeMott also offered encouragement. To all, the authors of the following essays extend their gratitude.

Peter S. Temes
Marblehead, Massachusetts
August, 1995

1

Can Leadership Be Studied?

Jacob Heilbrunn

In 1879 the young New England conservative Henry Cabot Lodge accepted for publication in the *International Review* a rousing essay calling for revived presidential leadership. Warning of the marked and alarming decline in statesmanship, the author lamented that "both state and national governments are looked upon with suspicion, and we hail an adjournment of Congress as a temporary immunity from danger" (10). The essay, which appeared at a time when the *Washington Post* could state as obvious that party bosses such as Thomas Reed of Maine were "no less consequential than the president," expressed a widespread unease among Americans over corruption in Congress and political drift.

More than a century later, Thomas Woodrow Wilson's essay, which he expanded into his best-selling book *Congressional Government* (1885), offers a reminder of the enduring preoccupation of Americans with leadership as well as the ambivalence with which they regard it. The yearning for decisive leaders and the apprehension that they might upset the balance between power and liberty has made Americans more adept at demanding leadership than at embracing it. Indeed, the U.S. Senate's defeat of Wilson's efforts to bring America into the League of Nations in 1920—a defeat engineered by the same Lodge who in 1879 had published Wilson's essay blasting congressional aggrandizement—could scarcely provide a more telling illustration of the constraints democratic leaders confront.

Today the renewed shift from international to domestic concerns has heightened the sense that we live in an age of pygmy figures hardpressed to cope with new events and challenges. The diverse interests at play make decisive leadership much harder to assert; the sway of "policy wonks" does not exactly elicit great passions. What is more, leadership itself continues to seem inimical to democratic virtues.

So perhaps it should not be altogether surprising that even the mere *study* of leadership has become the target of various broadsides. Writing in a recent issue of *Harper's*, Benjamin DeMott, a professor of humanities at Amherst College, depicts the entire enterprise of leadership studies as a racket cooked up by academics to swindle American taxpayers and the federal government. Recounting his service on an academic grant-review panel in Washington, DeMott tells how he "was introduced to the leadership-studies cult, a no-less-perfect specimen of late-20th-century academic avarice and a precise depth gauge of some recent professorial descents into pap, cant, and jargon." Though most of his essay is a demolition job, DeMott concludes his attack on a somewhat pious note, charging that the very idea of leadership studies carries with it an antirepublican, mugwumpish fear of the masses that dilutes our "democratic essence."

In truth, it is not difficult to detect a whiff of intellectual snobbery emanating from DeMott and other foes of leadership studies—even a hint of antidemocratic hauteur. After all, exposing high school and college students around the nation to ideas about leadership, as well as busing them into Washington to visit the State Department, Pentagon, and Congress, is in the best American egalitarian tradition. What could be more reflective of the American creed than the conviction that almost anybody can become—or be taught to be—a leader?

No doubt the breezy how-to tips contained in tracts such as *A Passion for Excellence* (1985) and *Leadership Secrets of Attila the Hun* (1985) inspire little confidence in the relatively youthful field. Still, it is easier to deride than to decipher the study of leadership. The recent efflorescence of leadership studies, including the creation of the Kennedy School's Leadership Project at Harvard University, the Jepson School of Leadership Studies at the University of Richmond, and countless other programs and projects throughout the nation, has produced its share of monsters, but the field has a more robust (and respectable) intellectual history than *The One-Minute Manager* (1982) might suggest. Theorists of leadership can point with pride to several solid accomplishments.

For a start, they have effectively addressed the question of leadership in public administration, business, and the military. The study of relations between workers and employers has, in fact, helped to improve those relations. Studies of "followership" and employee "empowerment" have been very useful to corporations forced to go through radical reorganizations by technological change and financial pressure. The faster that corporate chieftains "flatten management," the more quickly employees at even the lowest levels of management must learn to "lead" themselves.

Most important, the field has attempted to counter what John Gardner, a founding chairman of Common Cause and a professor at Stanford Business School, aptly called America's "anti-leadership vaccine." This vaccine, he charged in a 1965 Carnegie Corporation report, not only makes most Americans unreasonably suspicious of all kinds of leaders but "immunizes a high proportion of our most gifted young people against any tendencies toward leadership." Leadership studies provides at least one needed antidote to what Brooks Adams at the turn of the century termed the "degradation of the democratic dogma."

The question looming over the field is whether it can fulfill its quest for devising a scientific formula of leadership. Though leadership specialists readily acknowledge their own shortcomings, their work continues to reflect many of the positivistic assumptions of early social scientists, above all the notion that human behavior and traits can be abstracted, defined, and even quantified. This reification of leadership (to purloin a fancy social-science term) may seem hopelessly naive, but the evolution of the field merits attention. To study the rise of leadership studies is to realize that its failures, as well as its successes, have advanced our understanding of an important phenomenon.

The scientific study of leadership originated in the work of one of the founding fathers of sociology, Max Weber (1864–1920). A polymath who came to the study of sociology via law, Weber set the questions of authority, status, and legitimacy in the context of religion, politics, and the military. Devoting great attention to the unresolved tension between leaders and bureaucracies, he grew convinced that an inexorable trend toward rationalization in every sphere of society made the role of leaders both more problematic and more important.

Weber formulated three "ideal-types" of leadership: the rational-legal, the rational-authoritarian, and the charismatic. The charismatic leader was the most unusual of the three, and the only one, Weber thought, who might counter the dispiriting effects of life in an overly bureaucratic and rationalistic world, what he called the "iron cage" of modernity. Indeed, it was Weber's fondest hope that such a leader, endowed with extraordinary, even superhuman, qualities, might be able to instill in his followers a sense of mission and moral purpose that a thoroughly demystified society no longer provides.

The notion of charismatic authority was espoused in different form by Weber's contemporary, Georg Simmel (1858–1918), a lecturer in philosophy at the Humboldt University of Berlin. A pioneer in the study of social interaction, Simmel postulated the existence of a "prestige leader" who commanded obedience by dint of unique personal qualities. Even more than Weber, Simmel stressed that the prestige leader could be understood only in the context of the intimate relationship between the leader and follower. Leadership did not consist of a body of received wisdom handed down from the heights of Mount Sinai but instead depended on the follower's perception of his leader. By refusing to appeal to the base instincts that united them and by transforming their expectations of leadership, said Simmel, a leader could create a new kind of reality for his followers.

Though different elements of Weber's (and Simmel's) ideas have informed each stage of the study of leadership, the one constant running through the field's history has been the urge to fashion typologies. Indeed, the scientific study of leadership itself can be divided into three phases. In the first, from the turn of the century to World War II, researchers set about identifying the traits of leaders in an attempt to demystify charisma itself. The second phase, which lasted from World War II until around 1970, focused on the behavior of leaders. The third and current phase centers on the interaction between leaders and followers.

The first phase began promisingly enough. In an effort to identify the charismatic traits that leaders presumably possess, researchers such as Charles M. Cox, a finance professor at Brigham Young University, carried out a battery of tests designed to measure personality and character. These tests examined qualities such as the intelligence, physical appearance, dynamism, and speaking skills of exceptional leaders. Many researchers looked for leadership traits among school children. Not too startlingly, the studies revealed that the traits correlating most significantly with leadership were originality, judgment, liveliness, and the desire to excel.

Without question, the most important review of the traits field was conducted in 1948 by Ralph Stogdill, a professor of management science and psychology at Ohio State University. After examining 120 trait studies, this diligent social scientist declared that no consistent pattern of traits could be detected among leaders. "A person does not become a leader by virtue of the possession of some combination of traits," Stogdill concluded, "but the pattern of personal characteristics of the leader must bear some relevant relationship to the characteristics, activities, and goals of the followers." Because these "trait studies" were unable to quantify leadership, they seemed to demolish the "Great Man" theory of history. Leaders, it turned out, were neither more intelligent nor vastly more energetic than the average person.

Even before Stogdill's conclusions were presented, the leadership field had begun to turn from identifying traits to examining the behavior of leaders, an explicitly psychoanalytic approach that was advanced by the enormously influential Yale University political scientist Harold Lasswell. Lasswell did not wholly abandon the interest in typology. After conducting a series of interviews with leading political figures, he concluded that three types existed: the Agitator, the Administrator, and the Theorist. But Lasswell's main interest was in the psychodynamics of leadership. He even devised a formula to explain what impelled potential leaders to mount the public stage: $p \} d \} r = P$, where p equals private motives; d equals displacement onto a public object; r equals rationalization in terms of public interest; and $\}$ equals transformed into; the result, P, is the political man. All one can say of this remarkable formula is that the ineffable has never before been so decisively pinned down.

Other theorists of leadership, including Stogdill, contended that two types of behavior marked successful leaders. One was oriented toward the accomplishment of tasks; the other toward good relations with employees. Employees might designate a task-oriented individual as a leader, but they never termed an exclusively employee-oriented one as such. Under Stogdill's direction, a number of studies carried out at Ohio State disclosed that the effective leader would not only show consideration for his subordinates but also supply them with the tools to complete their tasks.

Identifying two main types of leadership behavior, however, was not the same as detecting precise patterns of interaction between leader and group. Even if the leader behaved in a considerate fashion toward his employees, his subordinates might remain dissatisfied with him. And there appeared to be no clear correlation between the behavior of the leader and the productivity of his employees. Stogdill and his associates were unable to draw a measurable connection between leadership style and performance. The behavioral studies demonstrated only that leadership behavior could profitably be grouped into two broad categories.

The third phase of leadership studies has attempted to examine those categories more closely, focusing on what might be called the "transactional" and "transformational" approaches. In the early 1970s, Edwin P. Hollander, a professor of psychology at Baruch College, employed the term "idiosyncrasy credit" to stand for the freedom that members of a group were granted to act idiosyncratically. He showed that a seeming paradox existed: Giving followers a measure of autonomy increased their willingness to respond to a leader's directions.

The stress on transformational and transactional styles was crystallized by the distinguished political scientist, James MacGregor Burns. Burns's massive study *Leadership* (1978) has, in fact, become the Rosetta Stone of recent leadership studies. Drawing on a wide range of historical examples and figures, from William Lloyd Garrison to Sir Robert Peel to Franklin Roosevelt, Burns offered an ambitious meditation on the nature of leadership, one that returned to Weber's and Simmel's emphasis on the leader-follower nexus. Unquestionably, Burns's most important insight was to draw a distinction between transformational and transactional leadership. Where transactional leadership is merely a version of managerialism that appeals to the economic self-interest of followers, transformational leadership alters the expectations of followers. Like Simmel and Weber, Burns contends that leaders can elevate their followers to new levels of morality and rectitude: "Moral leadership emerges from, and always returns to, the fundamental wants and needs, aspirations and values of followers."

The current generation of leadership theorists has not been slow to attempt to turn Burns's emphasis on the ineffable qualities of leadership into a measurable theory—or even to challenge it. Prominent among these challengers is Bernard Bass, a student of Stogdill's and a professor of organizational behavior at the State University of New York, Binghamton. The author of numerous books, including *Leadership, Psychology, and Organizational Behavior* (1960) and *Leadership and Performance Beyond Expectations* (1985), Bass contends that Burns created a wholly artificial distinction between transactional and transformational leaders. Far from being antithetical, the two types of leadership can exist in the same person. Leaders such as Charles de Gaulle, Franklin Roosevelt, and Lyndon Johnson displayed varying degrees of transactional and transformational qualities. By the same token, Bass points out, a leader may exhibit neither set of qualities.

In an attempt to refine further the understanding of transformational leadership, Marshall Sashkin, an adjunct professor at George Washington University, has devised a "Visionary Leadership Theory" to take account not only of the practices of leaders but also of the effect of their behavior on the culture of an organization. Sashkin argues that followers are transformed because they internalize the values of the organization. The task of the leader is to disseminate the organization's principles and to enunciate the values that animate the organization. The ultimate paradox, Sashkin finds, is that the effective transformational leader can employ a managerial approach in order to transform his followers.

Perhaps the most successful promoter of the transformational model in the business world is Warren Bennis, a professor of management at the University of Southern California. And not only in business: Vice President Albert Gore has reportedly made Bennis's *On Becoming a Leader* (1989) recommended reading for his advisers. Blunt in manner, Bennis decries "management education" and calls for the training of leaders. "Leaders conquer the context... while managers surrender to it," he says. Even though Bennis's books come close to the homiletic school of leadership writing, he deserves considerable credit for linking leadership theory to the challenge of global competitiveness.

Despite its successive adoptions of new approaches to the question of authority, the field of leadership studies has remained hobbled by its epistemological commitments. The scientific quest for a generic model of leadership can take one only so far. Employing factor analysis to quantify leadership and focusing so minutely on the qualities of leadership, the field repeatedly loses sight of one of the principal reasons for its subject's essentially unpredictable nature—the environment in which leaders function. Or, to put it another way, leadership studies lacks an adequate concern for context, historical or situational.

Is it no mystery that different times call for different kinds of leaders. In the business world, patient, low-profile managers are sometimes preferable to forceful visionaries. The energetic Lee Iacocca functioned best when he was leading Chrysler out of financial disarray. A similar rule obtains in the world of politics. Winston Churchill was ejected from office once he had fulfilled his mission of winning World War II. Leaders, of course, are usually incapable of reconciling themselves to the fact that they can leave an imprint only when a certain constellation of historical forces is present. After a friend commiserated with Churchill and told him his defeat at the polls was a blessing in disguise, Churchill muttered, "If it is, the disguise is perfect."

Besides scanting the historical dimension, leadership studies neglects the variety of arenas in which different kinds of leaders operate. Successful captaincy in business, government, or the military does not necessarily transfer to other fields—or even among those three. General Ulysses S. Grant made a terrible president. Moreover, thanks to academic neglect, we are largely clueless as to what makes a strong religious leader, culture leader, reform leader, intellectual leader, sports leader.

One scholar who has stepped into the breach is Gary Wills, a professor of humanities at Northwestern University. In his book *Certain Trumpets: The Call of Leaders*, Wills examines 17 kinds of leaders to show that a "leader whose qualities do not match those of potential followers is simply irrelevant." For each kind of leader, Wills chooses an ideal-type and an antitype to bring home his point that even an outstanding figure in a certain field is not necessarily a leader. He explains, for example, why the brilliant Viennese philosopher Ludwig Wittgenstein never became the kind of intellectual leader that Socrates had once been. ("Wittgenstein's theories were largely wrested out of himself in periods of seclusion, or while serving in the army, or in menial jobs. . . . He was a Socrates in intent without the theory or the methods that lent themselves to interactions with others.") Wills's book is noteworthy precisely because of the emphasis he puts on the ways various fields of human endeavor call forth very different kinds of leaders, an emphasis that the formal study of leadership would do well to take up.

Then there is the matter of elites and leadership. Contrary to DeMott's charge that leadership studies is elitist, the field shows inadequate concern for those networks through which leaders rise and operate.

The power of elites is particularly apparent in political arrangements, democratic as well as authoritarian, and the United States is no exception. National power continues to reside in institutions that promote elites—New York and Washington law firms, philanthropic foundations, the Ivy League colleges, the top media organizations. Though the power of these institutions should not be demonized, it is worth noting that at least half of the nation's industrial assets belong to 100 corporations, 50 foundations control 40 percent of foundation assets, and 25 universities control two-thirds of all private endowment funds in higher education. Fifty-four percent of corporate leaders and 42 percent of government leaders are graduates of 12 private universities—Harvard, Yale, Chicago, Stanford, Columbia, MIT, Cornell, Northwestern, Princeton, Johns Hopkins, Pennsylvania, and Dartmouth. That these institutions have opened their doors to minorities and women does not vitiate their importance as creators of elites; to the contrary, it vindicates their power. Again and again, elites in the United States, like the British establishment, have replenished their ranks, and these elites continue to set the course of the nation, for better or worse. Consequently, when things go wrong with the system, the problem is not simply the figure at the top. The quick fix of leadership (narrowly defined) cannot be dumped into the stalled engine of government like antifreeze; the deeper problems rest in the clash of interests and elites on issues such as health care and welfare reform.

Another question to which leadership studies could profitably direct more attention is where our leaders are ending up—and, just as important, why they end up where they do. As former Harvard president Derek Bok notes in his excellent book *The Cost of Talent* (1993)—which could just as fittingly be titled *The Cost of Leadership*—for the past 25 years the best students have shunned government service and teaching in favor of law, medicine, and business. Law and business schools boomed between 1970 and 1990, while only 1 percent of top students in elite universities opted to teach in public schools. Quite clearly, we get leaders where we put our money, though money is not the only factor. Prestige counts. Whatever the incentives, if those to enter government and education remain grossly disproportionate to those offered by the corporate and legal worlds, our most important public institutions will continue to suffer from lackluster guidance. Leadership studies might provide a valuable service by showing how other societies have encouraged leaders to seek careers in fields that serve the public interest.

For all its concern with leaderly qualities, the science of leadership has devoted too little attention to what might be called the darker side of the question. Ruthlessness, mendacity, dishonesty, and cunning—all are qualities that the leadership theorists flinch from. A promising start would be to return to the Weberian conception of charisma, which has lost none of its explanatory power. The interaction between charisma and paranoia, as the MIT political scientist Lucian Pye has noted, can form one of the more important characteristics of dictatorial leaders. The defense of a "homeland" or "party" against diabolical foes can increase a leader's charismatic appeal. It helps to explain why Stalin's and Mao's murder of millions did nothing to damage—and, indeed, increased—their mystique at home and abroad.

The mystery of leadership touches on some of the more vexing philosophical questions about human existence, which theorists ignore only at the risk of ultimate irrelevance. To date, the study of leadership has successfully identified many important traits of leaders and made valuable contributions to our understanding of how leaders and followers in organizations interact. But to grow as a discipline, it will have to cast a wider net. Doing so, it may discover that the most important things about leadership lie far beyond the capabilities of science to analyze.

Works Cited

Bass, Bernard M. *Leadership, Psychology, and Organizational Behavior.* New York: Harper, 1960.

———. *Leadership and Performance Beyond Expectations.* New York: Free Press, 1985.

Bennis, Warren G. *On Becoming a Leader.* Reading, MA: Addison-Wesley, 1989.

Blanchard, Kenneth, and Spencer Johnson. *The One-Minute Manager.* New York: Morrow, 1982.

Bok, Derek. *The Cost of Talent.* New York: Free Press, 1993.

Burns, James MacGregor. *Leadership.* New York: Harper & Row, 1978.

DeMott, Benjamin. "Choice Academic Pork: Inside the Leadership-Studies Racket." *Harper's* (December 1993): 61–77.

Lasswell, Harold Dwight. *Power and Personality.* New York: W. W. Norton, 1948.

Peters, Tom, and Nancy Austin. *A Passion for Excellence: The Leadership Difference.* New York: Random House, 1985.

Pye, Lucian. *Aspects of Political Development.* Boston: Little, Brown, 1966.

Sashkin, Marshall, and William R. Lassey, eds. *Leadership and Social Change.* 3e. San Diego: University Associates, 1983.

Simmel, Georg. *Conflict: The Web of Group Affiliations.* Tr. Kurt H. Worlff and Reinhard Bendix. New York: Free Press, 1964.

Weber, Max. *On Capitalism, Bureaucracy and Religion: A Selection of Texts.* Tr. Stanislav Andreski. Boston: Allen & Unwin, 1983.

Wills, Gary. *Certain Trumpets: The Call of Leaders.* New York: Simon & Schuster, 1994.

Wilson, Thomas Woodrow. *Congressional Government.* Boston: Houghton Mifflin: 1885.

2

Antipodes: Plato, Nietzsche, and the Moral Dimension of Leadership

Paul F. Johnson

"Leadership" is a word that, like "friendship" or "compassion" or "hope," strikes the ear with a deeply affective resonance and produces a mood of acceptance, or complicity—in any event a positive response. Our language is replete with morally charged terms, positive (like the ones just mentioned) and negative (like "dictator," "avarice," "anxiety"), that we employ every day without so much as a thought. But leadership itself is a profoundly ambiguous phenomenon and the liability is that we shall let the affective connotations attached to the word obscure the darker potentialities of the thing itself. It simply won't do, as some scholars have attempted, to define leadership in such a way as to preclude its being used to denote the practices of those whose effect upon the people who fall under their influence is harmful or otherwise untoward. We need, rather, to bring all forms of leadership under scrutiny and to incorporate into our analysis of its various methods and manifestations a specifically moral-theoretic component.

One of the more compelling aspects of leadership studies as a nascent academic discipline is the way its subject matter lends itself to treatment from a broad range of perspectives. Leadership is an empirical phenomenon conducive to study from a descriptive, social scientific, and value-free standpoint. As such, it is aptly approachable through the methods of sociology, psychology, and political science (among others). It is also an inherently humanistic concern whose ambiguities, contextuality, and normativity require the interpretive methods and devices of history, literature, and philosophy (among others). No account of leadership can be complete, or completely adequate, unless it makes some explicit attempt to integrate these two methodological perspectives. The challenge in trying to effect a more synoptic view of leadership revolves around the question of what to do with the ethical or moral aspects of leadership practice. Scholars of all disciplinary stripes have put their shoulder to the leadership wheel, and leadership studies seems willing to accommodate both the empirical and normative approaches. Very little attention has been paid so far, however, to the specific task of defining the moral issue in terms conducive to better cooperative effort.

In Plato and Nietzsche I find statement of two of the most powerful philosophical alternatives available to us in trying to deal with the inherently moral dimension of leadership. With Plato, we encounter the strategy of seeking after an independent, and in some sense universal standard of moral value by appeal to which any given instance of leadership practice may be assessed. In his *Republic*, by far the most familiar of his dialogues, he articulates this standard under the concept of the Form of the Good. Despite the various objections that have been raised concerning the nature or existence of the whole realm of the Forms, Plato's effort remains instructive because it helps us to understand the philosophical complexities involved in any approach to leadership that would be exhortatory, morally uplifting, or even critical. Any attempt to mark a normative difference between types of leadership practice requires some such moral standard as Plato attempts to articulate, and the value of bringing Plato into our conversation is that his approach to the problem represents one of the few viable strategies that has retained interest across the ages and offers perhaps the best prospect of achieving acceptable results. It is a subtle and arduous task, but with Plato we come into possession of a philosophical vocabulary and conceptual framework whereby the problems can be made tractable. With Nietzsche, one is spared such exertions. The moral sensibilities of a people and the leadership practices that we might find in place and operating in their midst are empirical factors which can be dealt with descriptively—whether we choose a psychological, a sociological, or evolutionary standpoint. Upon those who would eschew the philosophical task imposed by taking the Platonic approach, Nietzsche forces the recognition that relations inherent in the leadership phenomenon are nothing more than manifestations of disparities of power. Any attempt, on the empirical view, to say which forms of leadership are to be preferred reduces to a statement of which forms of power one prefers. Those preferences, advanced without any appeal to traditional or transcendent moral standards, are only too likely to be disguised expressions of group- or self-interest. Nietzsche's philosophy helps us to clarify the logic of any such value-free approach to the questions surrounding leadership.

There are, essentially, two directions we can take in trying to make sense of the moral element in leadership, the transcendent and the reductive. Each of these directions permits a variety of disciplinary perspectives, basic assumptions about human nature, and methodological devices. One needn't accept the specific doctrines of either Plato or Nietzsche, but one can scarcely avoid moving in one or the other direction which their philosophies define. Plato and Nietzsche stand at the two extremes—at the antipodes of moral discourse—and define, between them, the framework of reference, the conceptual space in which our evaluation of leadership practices must be situated.

Though the upsurge of interest in leadership studies is recent, the concern for the inherently moral aspects of leadership is not. It is, in fact, ancient. On the opening page of Plato's *Republic* we find the following exchange between Socrates, who is beginning a long walk back to Athens from the port of Piraeus, and Polemarchus, who with his friends would have Socrates tarry for some conversation:

> Polemarchus: Socrates, it looks to me as if you had started on your way back to the city.
> Socrates: Quite right.
> Polemarchus: Do you see how many we are?
> Socrates: Of course I do.
> Polemarchus: Well, you must either be stronger than we are, or you must stay here.
> Socrates: Is there not another alternative, namely that we may persuade you to let us go?
> Polemarchus: Could you persuade men who do not listen?

From the very beginning, as this passage makes clear, Plato has in view the alternatives of force and persuasion as the basis for human interaction.

Plato wrote the *Republic* in approximately 380 B.C., some 19 years after his chief protagonist Socrates was tried and executed by the citizens of Athens. At the time, Athens was ruled under a democratic form of government, though a direct and not a representative form. Proposed laws were considered in the Assembly and voted on by as many of the free males as could attend the frequent meetings. Any citizen with voting rights (and these were the minority of persons living under the Athenian regime) could propose legislation, and prospects for passage depended to a very large extent on the sponsor's ability to speak eloquently in support of it. The Greeks loved a good speech delivered in full-throated eloquence, and were not disposed to letting the substance of a proposed law stand in the way of valorizing the effective speaker with an affirmative vote. Nor were the members of the Assembly the least bit reserved in making known their disapproval of anyone whose rhetorical skills fell short of the style and flourish they expected. Under such conditions, it is only too easy to confuse the merits of a proposal with the eloquence of its sponsor, a tendency not lost upon those who would use the Assembly as a means to their personal aggrandizement. The ability to speak well and persuasively in the Athenian Assembly was thus a highly important skill for anyone who might care to seek personal gain through political means. There were no fewer of these in Athens than there are, say, in the United States of the late twentieth century.

Textbook economics tells us that where there is a demand for something a supply will be found, and to meet the demand for training in the arts of eloquent speech there arose in Athens a whole class of itinerant instructors of rhetoric who, for a price, would vouchsafe the various techniques and stylistic devices that might enable one to seduce an unsuspecting audience into acceptance of whatever point of view one might choose to advance. These were the *Sophists*, among whose leading lights we find such men as Protagoras, Gorgias, and, one of the important characters in the *Republic*, Thrasymachus. It was of no concern to the Sophists themselves what use their students might make of the skills they learned at their workshops. Whether the power of rhetoric were put to a good or a malicious use, in service of a just or a bigoted cause was irrelevant: the point was to *succeed*. It was, in fact, to the professional interests of the Sophists to deny that any clear distinction could be drawn between justice and injustice because, if that line could be drawn, the question regarding the relative effectiveness of one's speech should have to be subordinated to the deeper issue concerning the legitimacy of one's cause. It would be more important, in other words, to learn where justice lies and to side with it than to aspire to victory in the name of a cause which was unjust. If there is no justice or injustice, then the question of who should prevail in a debate must be decided on other grounds, and rhetorical power is as valid a standard as any. And that means clients for the Sophists. They might have done well to take as their motto: Pay up, learn the trade, go forth, and flourish. *They* certainly did flourish: or should I say "do," for the Sophists we have always with us.

To Plato's way of thinking the Sophists constituted a grave threat to the continued health of the Athenian city-state (or *polis*, the Greek term from which we derive "politics"). Wherever the interests of the polis conflicted with the interests of one of its citizens, the advantage fell all too often to the latter in public debate, that is to say, in the Assembly, if only he had had the foresight to learn what the sophists had to teach. Worse than that, on Plato's view, the obfuscation and ambiguities which sophistic teachings generated as they leached out into the general population led to a diminution of what we might call "civic-mindedness," to a decay in the citizens' own sense of owing a loyalty to their city that might require them to place their own personal interests in abeyance. It is not necessarily the case, as the Sophists themselves were quick to point out when they were suspected of this insidious influence, that the ability to speak well should always be put in the service of personal gain but, human nature being what it is, the temptation often proves too much for even the most public-spirited of persons. Plato recognized the pernicious aspect and the catastrophic potential of the Sophists' teaching, and he also discerned the most effective line of attack against them. The power of eloquent speech and rhetorical finesse would be undercut if people were shown that matters of public policy could be decided on more substantive and meaningful grounds. What is required for this showing is that there be a criterion by appeal to which the justice or injustice of a given proposal or cause could reliably be decided. We need to be able to say, in other words, *what justice is and how we come to know it*. These are the topics, precisely, that Plato means to address in the pages of *Republic*, and it was for the sake of challenging the influence of the Sophists in Athens that he set about its composition.

The *Republic* is, of course, a dialogue in which Socrates as the protagonist engages in an inquiry with some of the brightest young men in Athenian society about the nature of justice and the question, what is the good life for a human being. It is no accident that one of the key disputants in the very early portion of the text is one of the most popular Sophists of the day, Thrasymachus, who, when asked what he thought, replied that "justice is nothing other than the advantage of the stronger" (338c). Thrasymachus' view is crude, though honest enough: he means by this claim that it is only right that superior, that is, more powerful persons should rise to the top, and that they would be justified in using whatever means they have at their disposal, including the force of eloquence, for attaining their ends. Indeed, the very fact that one has ascended to a position of power indicates the legitimacy of one's exercising its prerogatives. It is one of the nicer dramatic embellishments of the text that the argument on behalf of force should be presented as a Sophist would present it: with intense rhetorical force.

Plato here reiterates the theme he introduced on the first page of the dialogue, the contest between persuasion and force, but now, by putting the advocacy of force into the mouth of a Sophist, he intends to show that eloquence, the efficacy of persuasive speech, is itself only a specific form of power. Two things can be said about Thrasymachus' view. First, he is an advocate of what might be called a natural hierarchy, claiming that, as a matter of natural fact, some people are stronger or smarter, in a word, more powerful than others. This is how nature has made us, and it is a reality obvious to anyone who looks. It is only natural, then, that a given human population will eventually sort itself into a vertical order with the more powerful toward the top and the less powerful falling into ranks beneath according to their relative strength among themselves. In saying that justice is "the advantage of the stronger" Thrasymachus means that this vertical ordering is how things *ought* to be, and again, that all persons are perfectly justified in using their powers in any way which conduces to their advantage. His view also implies, second, that the political order exists as a competitive field on which the struggle to the top, the contest between the relative strengths of individuals, can be played out. The name of the game is maximization of personal interests, and politics is only another means to this universal goal. And one of the most powerful instruments in the arsenal of self-interest is rhetoric, eloquence, *effective* speaking.

One of the cardinal teachings of the Sophists as a group derives from the famous dictum of Protagoras, perhaps the greatest of the Sophists: "Man is the measure of all things. . . ." It is normally understood that "man" here denotes the collective, "humankind," and asserts that we together bear within ourselves the standard of all valuations. But his assertion continues, ". . . of the things that are that [or 'how'] they are and of things that are not that [or 'how'] they are not." What Protagoras seems to have meant is not that humankind as a whole is the standard-bearer of value, but rather that each individual person is the sovereign judge of how things are, and what things have value. Protagoras is an advocate of what we would call relativism, and relativism of a rather comprehensive sort extending to cognitive and aesthetic perceptions as well as moral valuations, and his view is a basic element of Sophists' teaching generally. Whether we consider sensory perceptions of warmth or coolness (the same gust of air is a refreshing breeze to one person, a chilling draft to another), the merits of a given piece of artwork, or the moral assessment that might be made of someone's conduct, the individual is the sole arbiter and is virtually incorrigible in his or her perceptions. It is this doctrine of the Sophists which underwrites their denial of any clear distinction between justice and injustice.

In its moral dimension what the Sophists' teaching entails is a rejection of the existence of any objective standard of right and wrong, and, to make matters worse, the emergence of the Sophists in Athens coincided with the slow deterioration of the guiding influence of the religious traditions of the time. The public festivals and rituals were still held, but no one took seriously the reality of the gods to whom obeisance was ostensibly paid. The moral guide rails which regulated conduct and informed the citizens' sense of community within Athenian society had grown decrepit, a development which lent added force to the sophistic teaching. Plato was not alone in his recognition of the impending danger to the continued viability of the Athenian culture, nor are the challenges of moral relativism unique to his historical circumstances. Indeed, in our own day we find writers and social commentators deploring the very same developments. The constant appeal to "traditional" or "family" values is almost always attended with expressions of disdain at the rampant individualism which has swept into seeming hegemony in Western culture. We no longer seem to have the abiding sense of shared values which are necessary for a genuine sense of community. Our political practices have fragmented into the vociferations of special interest pleading, each group trying to secure their interests to the disregard of others. Our own sense of loss, disorientation, and anxiety for the future is much the same as Plato's in his day. Our situation is not at all dissimilar.

Listen, for example, to Joseph Rost as he describes the context in which his own attempt to construct a new model of leadership is made:

> With only the language of individualism to use and with only an interest accommodation model to inform that language when it comes to making decisions about changes in our organizations and societies, the people in the United States are without both the language and the moral systems of thought necessary to make morally coherent judgments about the content of leadership—proposals that indicate the real changes leaders and followers intend for our organizations and societies. (176)

His mention here of the *language* of individualism is especially noteworthy because it points to the fact that it is, after all, the language that we use amongst ourselves which embodies our moral sensibilities and translates them into public action. If there are no external moral standards, no criteria beyond our personal view of what is in our best interests, then Thrasymachus is probably right in counseling us to hone our rhetorical skills into more effective instruments for their pursuit. Or again, listen to the words of contemporary philosopher Alasdair MacIntyre as he decries the collapse of traditional moral values and their replacement by the ethics of individuality (a phenomenon he labels "emotivism"):

> [E]motivism entails the obliteration of any genuine distinction between manipulative and non-manipulative social relations. . . . If emotivism is true . . . evaluative utterance can in the end have no point or use but the expression of my own feelings or attitudes and the transformation of the feelings and attitudes of others. I cannot genuinely appeal to impersonal criteria, for there are no impersonal criteria. I may think that I so appeal and others may think that I so appeal, but these thoughts will always be mistakes. The sole reality of distinctively moral discourse is the attempt of one will to align the attitudes, feelings, preferences and choices of another with its own. Others are always means, never ends. (22, 23)

Thrasymachus is smiling.

In light of our present circumstance, it may be well to inquire how Plato proposed to address the dangers he perceived. The ensuing arguments of the *Republic*—comprising the remaining nine books of the dialogue—are devoted to establishing the reality of just such an external standard of morality as is required to defeat the claims of Thrasymachus and, by extension, the ethics of individualism which both Rost and MacIntyre deplore. Plato is the philosopher of moral objectivism par excellence, and his strategy in establishing the reality of the moral standard and articulating its nature involves three separate, but of course closely related themes.

The first theme has to do with the essentials of human nature. In *Republic* Plato sets forth his theory of the "tripartite soul," the coexistence within each of us of three distinct elements which he calls the rational, the spirited, and the appetitive. For present purposes what is important here is that reason is the most important, most "noble" faculty within us by virtue of the fact that it alone can put us into contact with what is *real*. The reality disclosed to reason is entirely distinct from the world we perceive through our senses, a world which is full of change and flux, never the same one moment to the next. The senses are generally reliable in informing us of such qualities as color or sound or smell, but the mistake is in thinking that these qualities are wholly constitutive of the real world. Their deficiency begins to show when we attempt to make comparative judgments among sensory perceptions, either between one perception and another within the same individual or between the perceptions of different persons. The same distance I walk on two consecutive days may seem to me very long and then very short, depending perhaps upon my mood; to two people walking side by side the distance to their destination may seem long to one, short to the other. But there is an objective fact of the matter concerning distance which can be measured mathematically. "How far?" is a question better answered with a number than with a subjective appraisal. But the pure magnitudes of mathematics (or, more appropriate to Plato's line of thought, geometry) are not things that we actually *see* at all, but rather are representative of a domain of reality to which we gain access only through the use of our reason. Large or small, weak or strong, fast or slow: these are all characteristics of the various entities and beings that we experience through sensory perception, and we make such comparative judgments every day. Plato's point is that such judgments concerning our perceptions are only objectively valid by virtue of our relating their sensory manifestation to a scale which is not itself sensory in nature. And if our perceptions are so very apt to change one moment to the next, and the perceptions of different people so apt to diverge, still, the rationally apprehensible domain of number and magnitude is itself enduring, immutable, and universally valid. These characteristics give this domain a higher ontological status than the world of impermanence and ambiguity revealed to our senses, and the reason within each of us which facilitates our awareness and knowledge of this domain can only be accorded a more noble and important status as well. Our opinions, which derive from our sensory perceptions of things, must always submit to correction from the higher knowledge attainable through reason.

The second dominant theme to emerge from the pages of *Republic* has to do with Plato's attempt to broaden the domain of rational knowledge to include not only mathematical magnitude but objective and universal measures which can be applied to our aesthetic and moral sensibilities as well. Corresponding to Plato's theory of human nature, and reason as the most ennobling element within us, we will find a theory concerning the nature of that reality to which our reason enables us to ascend, the Theory of Forms. When we look at a canvas of Monet, to begin with an example, we see not only the blues and greens and reds but also the *beauty* of the painting as well. Just as in the case of distance where mathematics enables us to place subjective determinants like "near" and "far" against an objectively valid framework, so too, according to Plato, there exists an objective measure for our aesthetic evaluation, the Form of the Beautiful. To one person in an art gallery the beauty of the Monet is simply arresting, while to the next person (let us suppose) it is entirely absent. We would be inclined to say in such a case that the aesthetic worth of the painting is entirely a matter of subjective taste. But for Plato, the question "how beautiful?" is exactly similar to the earlier question "how far?": it is a matter that must be decided by appeal to an objective and universally valid measure. The Form of the Beautiful is, like mathematical quantity, a reality which exists independently of the objects to which we might be inclined to apply the term "beautiful." It is not something we can see with our eyes, or, in the case of music with our ears. It is something known only to reason in the distinctively pristine mode of its knowledge, and it is by virtue of the fact that our minds are able to attain knowledge of the Form itself that we can recognize whether or to what extent a given artifact partakes of (Plato's locution is "participates in") the nature of this ethereal Beauty. The modern consciousness recoils from this hypostatization of aesthetic value, but even though you and I might profoundly disagree as to whether Stravinsky's *Rite of Spring* is beautiful, we both would claim to have some pretty clear idea of what it is that we are disputing about. The very possibility of our disagreeing seems to imply the reality of the standard to which we both appeal, and this is Plato's point. We must have some prior knowledge of what "the beautiful" is before we can dispute about the relative merits of the things our senses present to us for adjudication. And that prior knowledge comes to us through reason as it penetrates further into the realm of the forms.

The same argument holds for our moral perceptions. The Form of the Good is, for Plato, as objectively real and useful and important as the Pythagorean Theorem, and just as we should have to appeal to the Pythagorean Theorem if we wished, for example, to divide a parcel of land accurately, so too we must appeal to the Form of the Good as an objectively valid principle when it comes to the question of parsing mine and thine and ours. Against Thrasymachus, Plato argues that "self-interest" is no more adequate a response to my questions regarding what is right and wrong, regarding the nature of justice, than my companion's response of "not far" would be if I ask her where Toledo is. The Form of the Good is the objectively real, rationally apprehensible and universally valid standard against which all of our subjective *moral* perceptions should have to be measured. Assessments of right and wrong, good and evil, justice and injustice cannot simply be referred to my personal sense of what is best for me, because I may be entirely mistaken about the extent to which those intuitions accord with this independently existing criterion.

But how do we come to know of the existence of this objective moral standard, or learn how to apply it in the affairs of human life? Plato's answers to these questions constitute the third major theme of *Republic*. He offers two responses concerning, first, the identification of those persons who are capable of such knowledge and second, the type of education necessary for them to attain it. While Plato maintains that all human persons have within themselves the rational element which is capable of such knowledge, it is not the case that all persons possess this capacity in equal measure. Each person represents a peculiar configuration of natural talents: one person has the ability for spatial representation and the dexterity that makes for a good carpenter or mechanic; another person is athletic and high-spirited; a third is gifted in mathematics. In the ideal city which Plato describes in *Republic*, in the Republic itself, we shall have need of all these people, and we need them to devote their efforts to cultivating the special form of excellence which their unique configuration of talents makes it possible for them to attain. But within our population there will also be those whose peculiar talent consists in the unquenchable thirst for knowledge of the forms and in the odd philosophic turn of mind which intuits their existence beforehand and makes it possible to put all other pursuits aside. We need to find out who among us possesses this talent, this rational capacity in the predominant measure necessary for the long and arduous process of education required of anyone who would devote her life to the pursuit of knowledge of the Good. We shall have to test our young people, subject them to all manner of temptation and distractions to find out whether this very special talent abides within them. Socrates advises, "Like those who lead young horses into noise and tumult to see if they're afraid, we must expose our young people to fears and pleasures, testing them more thoroughly than gold is tested by fire" (413d). We shall have to give them every opportunity to pursue their pleasure or to shun personal danger in order to see whether they have within them the ability to subordinate the obstreperous claims of appetite and aversion to the tacit recognition of something higher which demands their allegiance. And what is it, precisely, that characterizes the person who possesses this ability? "We must choose . . . those men[1] who, upon examination, seem most of all to believe throughout their lives that they must eagerly pursue what is advantageous to the city and be wholly unwilling to do the opposite. [W]e must observe them at all ages . . . to make sure that neither compulsion nor magic spells will get them to discard or forget their belief that they must do what is best for the city" (412d–e).

The mark of the true leader for Plato, or rather, the defining capacity of a person who is suitable for training in leadership, consists in the intuitive grasp of the need to subordinate one's personal interests to the requisites of one's community. On Plato's view, this reflects the existence within such a person of a rational element more capacious and vigorous than the appetitive element with its interminable demands for pleasurable things and the avoidance of discomfiture. But the mere presence of this predominating element is not sufficient. It must also be trained in the appropriate way. The education of such young people who demonstrate their possession of reason in adequate proportion must begin with a rigorous study of geometry and mathematics so as to attune their minds to the existence of the immutable realm of ideas, the forms. They will be trained in music and made to see how the underlying mathematical structure of harmony informs the beauty of musical composition. They will be instructed in astronomy and shown how the universe itself accords with the elegance and symmetry and permanence of mathematical proportion. In all of this training they become gradually accustomed to seeing all things in the light of the forms and capable of interpreting all sensuous phenomena under their guidance. And they grow capable, in the fullness of time, of perceiving the form of the Good itself which stands paramount in the rational order of the forms. The few who ascend to these heights distinguish themselves as worthy of being the true guardians of the city, the genuine leader, because they alone are in possession of the knowledge required to say wherein consists the good of the city as a whole.

These three primary doctrines, then, the tripartite division of the soul, the theory of Forms, and a theory of education tailored to fit the reality of the Forms, constitute Plato's answer to the corrosive teaching of the sophists, with their moral relativism and the attendant valorization of the pursuit of self-interest—in short, the ethics of individualism. According to Plato, the only effective antidote to the insidious influence of the Sophists within the polis is the recognition of a moral standard independent of the subjective perceptions of the individual.

It may be helpful at this point to show how the philosophical strategy involved in Plato's moral theory pertains to the issue of leadership in our own day. In his important recent book, Joseph Rost offers a chapter on the ethics of leadership. In elucidating the ethical or moral issues which he recognizes to be intrinsic to the question of leadership, Rost asks us to make a careful distinction between these very terms, "ethical" and "moral." Rost "insist[s] that the ethics of leadership be included in the definition. The ethics of leadership has to do with the process of leadership—the relationship that is leadership—and not with the content of leadership, not with the question of whether such and such changes that certain leaders and followers intend are morally uplifting" (127). The process of leadership, the "leadership relationship" itself, can never be coercive or manipulative but must be based solely on persuasion, mutuality of purpose, and reciprocity of agency. It is these normative criteria which go to the ethics of leadership. But, Rost also insists, "Including a moral requirement in either the definition of leadership, or an understanding of transformation is too limiting, and thus unacceptable. There are no moral criteria in the postindustrial definition of leadership" (124). The moral question, then, goes to the specific changes towards the effecting of which the leadership group might direct its energies.

The problem, of course, is that what Rost is calling the "ethics" and the "morality" of leadership cannot be so neatly separated, either in theory or in practical application. How truly ethical can the cooperative intra-group relations be when their common purpose is depraved? And wouldn't non-ethical means be justifiable in cases where genuinely moral objectives were met with indifference or contempt on the part of those whose cooperative efforts were needed for their attainment? It is not obvious in the former case that such cooperative effort, no matter how congenial and reciprocative, should be described as leadership, nor in the latter that precisely the coercive attempt to get people to do the right thing should not count as leadership.

Having introduced this distinction, however, Rost does not propose simply to dispense with the moral element of leadership as here defined. In his chapter "Leadership and Ethics in the 1990s," he offers suggestions as to how the moral aspect of leadership should be addressed and where its nexus is most appropriately to be located. If the "ethics" of leadership has to do with the process—the internal means by which a group pursues its objectives—then "morality" has to do with the "content" of leadership, that is, the specific changes the group seeks to make in their social environment. Rost seems clear enough that the ethical question is intrinsically tied to the moral one, which is to say that the task of assessing the ethicality of a leadership group is not complete until there has been some further evaluation made of the ends this group intends to pursue. He writes:

> An ethical framework of leadership content requires that leaders and followers use a moral standard of the common good to make ethical judgments about the real changes they intend for organizations and societies.... What is needed is a reconstitution of our understanding as leaders and followers of the concept of civic virtue, the elemental notion that all of our goods as individuals and groups are bound up in the common good, or, to put it another way, that all of our self- and group interests are bound up in the public interest. (174, 176)

When Rost goes on to call attention to the "need to be able to think about the ethics of leadership content as a community," and the "need to develop a second language that will enable us to talk about the common good of the community," we could do worse than to place ourselves under the tutelage of Plato who addressed a similar need in a time not so very dissimilar to our own. Rost, indeed, is a Platonist in these two respects: that he believes that there is such a thing as the "common good," and that some form of rational inquiry, or persuasive speech, is the means through which we may come to know what it is. The third element in the Platonic theory is not explicit in Rost, but it is there by implication: that reason will enable us to subordinate our own interests and desires to those of the community in the event that they conflict (as invariably they do). Plato offers us a first attempt to develop the moral language which Rost calls for as crucial in our attempt to address the parlous situation into which we have fallen, and the enduring power and attraction of Plato's thought, and his importance for all students of leadership consists in the clear articulation which he brings to the moral intuitions which he shares, across the ages, with all persons who care about the moral substance of their society.

Two essential elements of Platonic moral theory—the special nature and office of reason and the moral standard which it enables us to know—have exercised an especially pervasive and enduring influence in the shaping of the Western mind. Through the writings of St. Augustine in particular, the Platonist vision was transposed in such a way as to provide support and leavening for the long tradition of Christian philosophy which begins with him. That is another story to tell, but suffice it to say at this juncture that Christianity itself partakes of the essential structure of Platonic moral theory owing to its appropriation of Greek philosophy at a crucial moment in its early history. While it can hardly be maintained that Plato's philosophy enjoys wide currency today, its fundamental insights continue to exert their influence by virtue of the fact that it retains a presence in the Christian approach to the question of morality. In its theological dimension, however, Christianity offers two significant advantages over Plato in its ability to account for the essential components we've adduced to this point. Reason itself can be explained as the presence within humankind of God's divine nature, and the Form of the Good can be explicated as the Will of God. Through these distinctive Christian doctrines, the moral experience of the West has been shaped and handed down in the form of a tradition of discourse which has hitherto provided the linguistic and institutional resources necessary to sustain our culture. But what happens when the theological doctrines which support the tradition of moral inquiry begin to lose their influence within society? As in ancient Athens, the religious substrate of contemporary Western culture seems to be in a state of disrepair, the foundations are crumbling, and our moral practices are called into question anew. One of the most important currents in the recent history of the West has been the slow erosion of confidence in the validity of the religious doctrines that have sustained us for so long.

One of the most formidable challenges to this tradition of theologico-moral inquiry comes at the end of the nineteenth century in the works of Nietzsche. Nietzsche was trained as a philologist and a classicist and was therefore entirely familiar with the historical and cultural predicament of Athens which we sketched above. He is also a philosopher of the first rank who offers us an important critique of the cultural values of the West and a wholly different conception of reason and morality. He stands poles apart—at the very antipodes—from the Platonic view of the matter, and in the present attempt to articulate the conceptual space in which our concerns for the nature of leadership must be situated, we begin with Nietzsche's own interpretation of the situation at Athens which, as we have seen, first inspired Plato to write *Republic*.

The historical situation under consideration is, Nietzsche writes, "a very remarkable moment."

> The Sophists verge upon the first *critique of morality*, the first *insight* into morality:—they juxtapose the multiplicity (the geographic relativity) of the moral value judgments;—they let it be known that every morality can be dialectically justified; i.e., they divine that all attempts to give reasons for morality are necessarily *sophistical*. . . . [T]hey postulate the first truth that a "morality-in-itself," a "good-in-itself" do not exist, that it is a swindle to talk of "truth" in this field.[2]

The Sophists, in other words, were on to something important. By raising the question of values as they did—and at the precise moment *when* they did—they put all of Athenian culture on the defensive by demanding that the social and political practices of the time be brought to account, that they *say* wherein consisted their legitimacy and justification. But cultural values generally are not the sort of thing which operate at the level of discursive argument. They tend, rather, to be unreflective, received on the authority of tradition, and they constitute the ground rules for a society which people are simply expected to abide if they wish to participate in the life of the society and enjoy the benefits which it confers. Edmund Burke makes this point in defense of tradition in the face of the French Revolutionary onslaught; Lytton Strachey mocks the cultural values of Victorian England with malicious glee by pretending to take up a position external to their operation. The same thing is at work in the United States at the present day, where the hue and cry has been raised over the decline of "traditional values," "family values," with the attendant sense of disorientation and defensiveness against an uncertain future. Returning to the case of Athens before Socrates, and again in Nietzsche's account,

> The dialectical manner was repudiated in good society; one believed it compromised one; youth was warned against it. [Socrates himself was convicted of corrupting the young.] Why this display of reasons? Why should one demonstrate? Against others one possessed authority. One commanded: that sufficed. Among one's own, *inter pares*, one possessed tradition, *also* an authority: and finally, one "understood one another"! One simply had no place for dialectic. Besides, one mistrusted such public presentation of one's arguments. Honest things do not display their reasons in that way. There is something indecent about showing all one's cards. (WTP 431)

This tacit "understanding" among a given population, this unreflective agreement about "how we do things" is what gives cultural values their special power. One never has to ask—indeed it is not clear that one *can* intelligibly ask—whether the practices they sponsor are right or just because it is only in relation to our shared values that we are able to say what righteousness and justice are. The peculiar force of the sophistic challenge, and its tendency to arise again and again in the course of history, is owing to the fact that cultural values are always more or less parochial in scope and serve to identify the interests of one group against the interests of others. When those others come to have a significantly large presence within the culture, one of two things can happen: they can assimilate, or they can call the operation of the cultural values into question. The Sophists represent the presence of "the other" in Athenian culture, and it was not their intention to assimilate.

In this light, Plato's strategy in contending against the Sophists becomes clear. Throughout the Platonic dialogues we find Socrates confronting prominent persons in Athenian society and asking them to define—that is, to give a discursive account of—the various virtues which they claimed to know and practice in their lives. In *Republic* the virtue in question is justice, but Socrates had also inquired into piety, courage, friendship, and any number of others, always tripping up the social bigshots, the lawyers and priests and politicians who were unfortunate enough to be buttonholed by him on the streets of Athens. These encounters always took place in the presence of a small troupe of young people (Plato himself among them) who took delight in seeing the authority figures of the day made to look foolish, dogmatic, unknowing. Prior to *Republic* Socrates/Plato seem able to come to no sure resolution of the questions, though taking it as progress that, at least, all parties to the exchange had come to realize that they did not know what they thought they knew. It is only with *Republic* and in subsequent dialogues that Plato begins to advance a coherent theory—the theory of Forms—which enables us to say what virtue really is. Reason, through the practice of Socratic dialectic, enables us to penetrate through the fog of cultural practice and gain entry into the world of the forms where we will find the standards of adjudication suitable for measuring the validity of those cultural practices. But, says Nietzsche,

> *In praxi*, this means that moral judgments are torn from their conditionality, in which they have grown and alone possess any meaning, from their Greek and Greek-political ground and soil, to be denaturalized under the pretense of sublimation. The great concepts "good" and "just" are severed from the presuppositions to which they belong and, as liberated "ideas" [forms], become objects of dialectic. One looks for truth in them, one takes them for entities or signs of entities: one *invents* a world where they are at home, where they originate.
>
> *In summa*: the mischief has already reached its climax in Plato.... (WTP 430)

The "mischief" to which Nietzsche alludes here is the deliberate (and on Nietzsche's view of Plato, disingenuous) attempt to make of moral values something that they are not and never can be. This moralizing tendency to seek after universally valid standards of adjudication appears at historical moments of great cultural distress, according to Nietzsche, and just as Athens had its Plato, so too Rome had its St. Paul and St. Augustine. Platonic and Christian moral teachings have this further similarity, then, that they attempt to provide a new moral foundation for a culture in decline. That these new moral visions should owe their birth to such historical contingencies does not detract from their power to reconfigure and revitalize a culture—indeed, for Nietzsche they are only too effective in securing a new moral order precisely because they are driven into cultural currency by a sense of urgency and desperation. The subliminal forces at work in their emergence and the ulterior motives that people have for accepting them only serve to obscure the deeper realities of the human condition which find expression in moral practices. It is for the sake of disclosing these deeper realities that Nietzsche undertakes his critique of Western or "European" values generally, and the Christian-moral world view in particular.

Nietzsche's critique of morality—at least, those aspects of it germane to present interests—is advanced along two different fronts. He intends, first, to contend against the conception of reason which makes of it a higher authority within the human person, taking as its function the ordering and subordination of the appetitive elements within the soul (to speak Platonese). And second, he challenges the legitimacy of the notion of a common good, that is, a moral condition of society in which the interests of all persons can be accommodated to as great an extent as is possible.

These two aspects of Nietzsche's critique have a common root. The individual human being is very similar to human society at large in that the individual comprises a vast multiplicity of interacting elements which strive for, but only intermittently achieve a condition of more or less stable equilibrium. Society itself is made up of disparate elements—both individuals and groups—which jostle and contend among themselves, and what we call "community" is, again, only a temporary compromise worked out in the accommodation of competing interests. In his attempt to articulate and describe the various components which make up both, Nietzsche will have recourse to a basic explanatory principle which he calls "the will to power." One virtue that Nietzsche claims in favor of this principle is precisely its ability to explain a very broad range of phenomena and to provide a common framework in the context of which seemingly diverse domains of inquiry can be integrated. Our task will be to show how the will to power provides an account for human nature in its individual and social dimensions which is antithetical to Plato's and yet enormously useful as an interpretive vantage point for the analysis of our current moral predicament.

It is a profound mistake, in Nietzsche's view, to think of reason as somehow possessed of a sovereign authority in the inner life of a human being. In order to reach an accurate understanding of ourselves we must begin at the level of physiology and recognize that the human organism comprises a complex and deeply intricate system of chemical and biological functions which are productive, at the level of consciousness, of certain instinctive drives and affective states.[3] What appears in consciousness is itself only a function of the various dispositions and states in which the body finds itself:

> In the tremendous multiplicity of events within an organism, the part which becomes conscious to us is a mere means. . . . The animal functions are, as a matter of principle, a million times more important than all our beautiful moods and heights of consciousness: the latter are a surplus, except when they have to serve as tools of those animal functions. The entire *conscious* life, the spirit along with the soul, the

> heart, goodness, and virtue—in whose service do they labor? In the service of the greatest possible perfection of the means (means of nourishment, means of enhancement) of the basic animal functions: above all, the enhancement of life.
>
> What one used to call "body" and "flesh" is of such unspeakably greater importance: the remainder is a small accessory. (WTP 674)

This vast multiplicity of organic functions and instinctual drives which Nietzsche posits as basic to the human constitution is not, of course, a chaotic maelstrom of wholly discrete and independently effective forces. The relative strength of each of these elements must exert itself over against the claims of the others, subordinating itself to more potent or more fundamental forces, and striving to gain expression above the clamor of the rest. Intelligence, or reason, is not, according to Nietzsche, a distinct element within this multiplicity but only the manifestation of the current state of its configuration. "We suppose," he writes, "that *intelligere* [understanding] must be something conciliatory, just, and good—something that stands essentially opposed to the instincts, while it is actually nothing but a *certain behavior of the instincts toward one another*."[4] What we experience at the level of conscious mental life is only the reflection of the relative state of equilibrium that has been achieved among the various drives engendered at the level of instinct and physiology. To suggest, as Plato does, that the mind, "reason," can somehow call the shots, or direct traffic among these enormously powerful and obstreperous forces is to put things exactly backward. To be sure, the mind or consciousness, as a factor within this systemic whole, may have an influence upon how the various forces come to be configured among themselves, but its influence never reaches anything like effective control. Nor does it make clear sense, on the view that Nietzsche presents, to think that reason is a discrete or independent element different in kind from the bodily functions. Mental states are essentially only body states manifest in a peculiar fashion.

One implication of this view of the human constitution provides a nice bridge to the second topic to be addressed, the nature of our social interactions. If there is within each one of us this vast welter of mutually influencing, and mutually contentious functions and drives, then it is very unlikely that any two of us will comprise the same forces in similar measure or that the elements that we *do* possess will come to rest in a stable state which resembles those of others. This claim has to do with the facts of physiology: one person's metabolism is faster than the next, one person has a larger lung capacity and hence a richer supply of oxygen to the blood, or greater brain mass or whatever. The factors involved here are immensely diverse, and the permutations of possibilities virtually infinite. Now, there is a sense in which this is trivially true—we are all different, each person is unique. Nietzsche, however, is intent on pressing this claim through to a more invidious conclusion which derives from the special features he imputes to the will to power. We have spoken of the condition of relative equilibrium toward which the plurality of interacting forces will tend in their contentious interaction, but this more or less stable state is not at all the final objective toward which they naturally tend, the natural end state of the organism itself. It is not a state of rest or containment, nor even the achievement of self-preservation toward which the vital life forces at work within us are directed. "The essential thing in the life process," Nietzsche asserts, "is precisely the tremendous shaping, form-creating force working from within which *utilizes* and *exploits* 'external circumstances'. . . . . Physiologists should think again before positing the 'instinct of preservation' as the cardinal drive in an organic creature. A living thing wants above all to *discharge* its force: 'preservation' is only a consequence of this" (WTP 647, 650).

All natural organisms are constituted of a multiplicity of elemental forces, and these forces will coalesce into that configuration which makes the organism maximally effective in exerting itself, as a discrete entity, within the environment it inhabits and against all the other organisms with which it comes into contact. Here is where the plot begins to thicken. Human beings are no different from other natural organisms in being constituted of a multiplicity of physiological functions and instinctual drives. Two aspects of the will to power, as the deeper philosophical principle which explains the nature of these vital forces, need to be made clear. First, we cannot isolate any one of these forces for the sake of independent inspection because, in Nietzsche's conception of the term, a "force" can only be identified in relation to the various resistances which it confronts. Or, looked at the other way, a given force is only the manifest resistance which stands in the way of another. "Force" and "resistance," in other words, are correlative terms and when we speak of a force we are actually referring to the presence of a duality (or plurality) whose very presence can only be discerned by virtue of the temporary stasis they achieve in each other's company. "The will to power," as Nietzsche has it, "can manifest itself only against resistances; therefore it seeks that which resists it . . ." (WTP 656). Second, the equilibriated state which an organism attains—and which we human beings experience in our conscious mental life—is only a sort of holding pattern to be maintained until such time as it—we—can find an opportunity to "discharge" the potential energy in a manner commensurate with the nature of the power to be discharged, that is, when a form of resistance is encountered which somehow matches it. By his very use of the term "will to power" Nietzsche intends to capture what he perceives to be the fundamental characteristic of all living organisms—indeed all natural phenomena: the primordial impulse of each "quanta of energy" to grow, to exert its dominance over less puissant quanta, to recombine with those of greater power and, in all events, to press outward in the constant effort to exert itself against others, attaining dominance in a temporary equilibriated state and then dissolving into ever new configurations in the contest with differently configured, more efficacious forms of combined force. That is how the world *is*.

Society itself represents a field within the context of which individual human beings collectively constitute the "multiplicity" of interacting forces. The same analysis which Nietzsche applies at the level of individual human nature—more specifically, in terms of physiology, biology, and psychology—is replicated at the level of society. All human relations, to draw a general conclusion at last, are relations of relative strength, of power, and there is no important distinction in kind to be drawn between our interactions and those of any other natural organisms. We are inclined and habituated to think that our interactions are distinctive because of our perceived need to comport ourselves under the guidance of moral law or social custom, aspects of our conscious life together which somehow set us apart from the natural order by virtue of the fact that morality itself partakes of a trans- or supernatural reality. But for Nietzsche, nature is all there is, there is no "other world" of Platonic forms, no spiritual realm. And *if* that is correct, then his reduction of moral phenomena to the level of physiology and biology can hardly be gainsaid. Nietzsche's whole philosophical project can be seen as the attempt to challenge and to dispense with all philosophical and theological doctrines which appeal to anything beyond nature, which impute to mankind some metaphysically distinct and transcendent characteristics which set us apart from, and above the natural order.

> For to translate man back into nature; to master the many vain and fanciful interpretations and secondary meanings which have been hitherto scribbled and daubed over that eternal basic text *homo natura*; to confront man henceforth with man in the way in which, hardened by the discipline of science, man today confronts the *rest* of nature, with dauntless Oedipus eyes and stopped-up Odysseus ears, deaf to the siren songs of old metaphysical bird-catchers who have all too long been piping to him 'you are more! you are of a different origin!'—that may be a strange and extravagant task but it is a *task*—who would deny that?[5]

What becomes of morality when it is cut loose from its metaphysical and theological moorings as Nietzsche insists it must be? What does a "naturalized morality" look like? "I understand by morality," Nietzsche writes, "a system of evaluations that partially coincide with the conditions of a creature's life" (WTP 256). To bring out the truly provocative aspect of Nietzsche's critique of morality, however, we need to introduce one further claim he makes with respect to human nature generally. As we have seen, we are all of us constituted by an agglomeration of vital impulses and physiological functions which ebb and flow, which coalesce into more or less stable configurations in accordance with resources available for exploitation and the environmental conditions we encounter, including the presence of others of our kind. According to Nietzsche, however, the relative degree of strength achievable by individuals is not uniform. There are some of us who comprise more vigorous and multifarious energies permitting of more efficacious configurations. In short, some people are stronger, more talented, industrious, etc., than others. Among the metaphysico-theological doctrines that must be jettisoned along the way to a naturalized morality is the idea that "all men are created equal." "My philosophy," Nietzsche tells us, "aims at an ordering of rank" (WTP 287).

There are, on his view, any number of "types" of human beings, distinguishable on the basis of their relative "quantum of energy," but for the sake of explicating the nature of morality these can be divided into two general types, the higher type and the herd type. What marks the difference is the extent to which an individual is capable of independent action, that is, the extent to which she can define goals for herself, marshal her strengths and contrive to "discharge" them in creative and "life enhancing" ways. The higher types are those who possess this capability in sufficient measure as to make for effective and autonomous agency in the world. The herd type is one who finds it necessary to cooperate with others in the attempt to achieve the goals that they agree among themselves are worthy of pursuit, a determination which is made on the basis of their perceptions regarding their relative strength as individuals. When Nietzsche says that a morality (and he is accustomed to speaking in the plural, of "moralities") is "a system of evaluations that partially coincide with the conditions of a creature's life," he means that the various "thou shalt's" and "thou shalt not's" which constitute a moral system are directed toward the suppression of conduct which pits the strength of one person over against the strength of others, and the facilitation of activities which tend to their mutual advantage *precisely by virtue of the fact that their efforts thereby become collaborative.* It is symptomatic of the herd type that the individual will scrupulously abide with the publicly acclaimed moral values and vociferate for their universal application for all members of the group, not because these have any transcendent or theological validity (although the individual will surely proclaim that they do) but only because he recognizes, tacitly to be sure, that to abide with the system and to try to get as many others as possible to comply with it establishes those social conditions under which his prospects of flourishing are maximized. Morality, then, as a system of valuations which sponsor and hold in place a set of practices or institutions, is a sort of subterfuge, a ruse which makes it possible for persons of similar endowments to get on with one another and to prosecute their mutual interests more effectively against a hostile and difficult world.

On these terms the whole question regarding the possibility of a "common good" is transformed. It is the function of "a morality" to serve the interests of a specific group, to consolidate a certain set of practices which conduce to the flourishing of a specific "type" of human being. In his naturalizing mode, Nietzsche does not argue for the wrongness or invalidity of any particular code of ethics, because he recognizes the subliminal power by which it exercises its influence upon the people drawn to it. This is especially true of the moralities tied to religious doctrines: "How much one needs a *faith* in order to flourish, how much that is 'firm' and that one does not wish to be shaken because one *clings* to it, that is a measure of the degree of one's strength (or, to put the point more clearly, of one's weakness). . . . For this is how man is: An article of faith could be refuted before him a thousand times—if he needed it, he would consider it 'true' again and again . . ." (GS 347). We are drawn to and compelled by conscience to adhere to those moral values which serve our interests in the world. The "herd morality" of which Nietzsche is so terribly derisive throughout his writings is directed to securing the interests of those individuals who are less strong, less autonomous, less able. Morality tends to settle at the level of the lowest common denominator, conducing to the interests of the weak, frustrating the higher ambitions of the strong. There can be no "common good" because there are different types of human beings whose conditions of flourishing and vital good health are different. The moral conditions which secure the well-being of one type are destructive of the higher type who has it within him to become something other, something more than the timid, well-mannered and altogether manageable specimen of humanity that thrives under the common code. The notion of a common good is contrary to the inherent impulses of life itself which seeks always after its own "enhancement" and expansiveness; it is contrary to nature, and anyway, its realization would come at too high a price.

This is strong medicine, to be sure, but there are, I think, important reasons for bringing Nietzsche into our conversation about the nature of morality as it applies to the question of leadership. The special power of Nietzsche's vision, of his attempt to "translate humankind back into nature" is to be found in the thoroughness with which all trace of the transcendent has been eliminated. Not only is there no appeal to theological or metaphysical notions of God, or the spiritual realm, or the world of forms; Nietzsche also offers an explanation of *why* theology and metaphysics hold such an enduring attraction for us in our attempts to understand ourselves. Nietzsche's philosophy offers us perhaps the most powerful vision of a world without God, and it challenges us to think carefully about our prospects of establishing a theory of morality on purely naturalistic grounds. If nothing else it forces us to recognize the implications, or perhaps more aptly, the *limitations* of a purely empirical approach to the leadership phenomenon.

Many contemporary writers have called attention to the connection between the increasing moral volatility of our time and the slow erosion of religious faith in the modern age. Their insight, while important, is hardly new. Writing in 1789, John Adams remarked, "Our Constitution is designed for a moral and religious people. It is wholly unfitted for any other." What happens, then, to a republic founded on religious principles (we are "created" equal, we are "endowed by our Creator" with certain inalienable rights, etc.) in which a sizable and increasing segment of the populace ceases to abide with the religious doctrines inscribed in its founding documents? On what do we now base our claims of equality? Where do we get our rights from? Our situation, again, is not so terribly different from the one we earlier described as having arisen in Athens. The gods, and the public rituals devoted to their honor and mollification, had ceased to inspire the allegiance of the public, and, had ceased, therefore, to provide the common framework of values which makes for a coherent and cohesive public order. Into the vacuum there stepped the sophists, who were only intent on taking seriously, as it now seems, the parochial nature of moral values generally and offering guidance as to how one should proceed in the interests of getting ahead under a changed cultural reality. When Thrasymachus avers that "justice is nothing other than the advantage of the stronger," he can be understood as setting a purely naturalistic standard of morality in the place of the erstwhile religious values. But nature, it turns out, and as Nietzsche forces us to realize, offers little help in marking the distinction between virtue and vice. Thrasymachus is only demanding that we call a spade a spade, and thereby gives voice to the dilemma into which Athenian society had fallen. Nietzsche does the same for contemporary civilization. Nietzsche himself congratulates the sophists for their insight when he writes, "every advance in epistemological and moral knowledge has reinstated the Sophists" (WTP 428). Thrasymachus, we might say, was the world's first Nietzschean.

He has hardly been the last. Indeed, Thrasymachus represents a point of view that has been a perennial temptation across the long history of moral discourse. Machiavelli and Hobbes, to cite two further examples, also give voice to the constant appeal which power has as a fundamental category of human interaction. It is, perhaps, not too much to say that there lies within the depths of human nature itself this darker potentiality which surfaces again and again in the course of history to challenge us to think anew about how, why—or even whether—the aggressive vital impulses of humanity should be constrained and put in the service of humane ideals. I have tried here to make the case that Plato and Nietzsche represent the antagonists whose antithetical visions have contended for ascendancy across our cultural history. The emergence of leadership as an especially compelling issue in contemporary life is really only the present-day manifestation of this perennial moral engagement.

I conclude by affirming what has perhaps already become clear to the reader: Leadership is a moral issue. As such it requires that we make use of the methods and conceptual tools that have always been the special concern of the humanities in general, and philosophy in particular. We need to develop a philosophy of leadership which sets moral theory at the center of things. All of the new ways of thinking about leadership, all of the innovative new techniques and skills that have been developed recently in any number of fields will stand to gain if we can articulate the matrix of moral possibilities which defines the range of alternative directions we may choose to pursue. Leadership always involves choices of a distinctively moral nature, and we must strive to develop the conceptual instruments which enable us to take our bearings within the moral space that lies open to us.

Notes

1. In Book Five, Plato argues extensively that it is not *only* men, males, who will have the desired characteristic. Women too will possess the rational capacity in question, and they too will be sought.

2. *The Will to Power*, translated and edited by Walter Kaufmann, section 428. All further references to this work will be cited in text as "WTP" followed by section number (not page).

3. For an especially intriguing—and largely corroborative—account of the relation between rationality and physiology (or somatic states) see Antonio Damasio, *Descartes' Error: Emotion, Reason, and the Human Brain*.

4. Friedrich Nietzsche, *The Gay Science*, translated by Walter Kaufmann, section 333. Again, all further references to this book will be made in text as "GS" followed by section number.

5. Friedrich Nietzsche, *Beyond Good and Evil*, translated by R.J. Hollingdale, section 230.

Works Cited

Damasio, Antonio. *Descartes' Error: Emotion, Reason, and the Human Brain.* New York: Putnam's, 1994.

MacIntyre, Alasdair. *After Virtue.* Notre Dame, IN: University of Notre Dame Press, 1981.

Nietzsche, Friedrich. *The Will To Power.* Tr. Walter Kaufmann. New York: Vintage, 1968.

———. *The Gay Science.* Tr. Walter Kaufmann. New York: Vintage, 1974.

———. *Beyond Good and Evil.* Tr. R. J. Hollingdale. New York: Penguin, 1973.

Plato. *The Republic.* Tr. G. M. A. Grube. Indianapolis: Hackett, 1992.

Rost, Joseph. *Leadership for the Twenty-First Century.* New York: Praeger, 1991.

3

"Leadership Studies": A Critical Appraisal

Daniel Born

1. Claims and Context

Claims about "leadership," like those of "quality" or "excellence," are made today with such numbing regularity and in so many institutional settings that generalization about a field called "leadership studies" may well be impossible, if not downright silly. Still, it is worth the attempt, particularly if we want to achieve some degree of self-reflexivity about the teaching and scholarship we do under its rubric.

Such a rubric, at least in this country, encompasses a variety of formal educational programs emerging in the last twenty-five years through a network of corporate foundations, liberal arts colleges, universities, and the military establishment.[1] In some cases special courses carry the "leadership" label; in other instances, there might be a certificate, a minor, a major (the Jepson School claims to be the first institution to offer a major, since 1992), or even a doctorate, such as that offered by the University of San Diego's School of Education. The U.S. Marine Corps training manual (1984) is dominated not by discussion of combat but by the theme of leadership, with lengthy sections devoted to "Foundations of Leadership," "Ethics and Leadership," "Leader and Follower," and "Philosophy of Leadership."[2] According to Bernard Bass, roughly 600 institutions of higher learning in America now offer some form of "leadership studies" in their curricula (xii), and if we include the military, as well as the myriad business and motivational seminars now offered under the leadership umbrella, then virtually everyone encounters some form of leadership doctrine in school or at work.

For a comprehensive account of the phenomenon of leadership studies, it will not suffice merely to trace particular theories. We must also seek to understand context: institutional constellations and funding sources which help incubate and bring theories to term.

Of crucial importance is the relationship between "leadership studies" and the liberal arts curriculum which for decades has been the training ground for many, if not most, leaders of every stripe—in business, government, the arts, science, and so forth. I find two disturbing trends where leadership studies and the liberal arts converge. These are: (1) a variety of anti-intellectualism in some leadership circles, and (2) a brand of unreflective communitarianism which celebrates groups and demonizes individuals. While my aim in this essay is not primarily to legitimate leadership studies, it seems to me that these two broad impulses, if left unchecked, will prove obstacles to the development of a vital field of research and debate.

The most disquieting tendency in leadership studies rhetoric is the subtle diminishment of academic work, even as the claim is advanced that leadership studies constitutes a new discipline complete with specialized vocabulary and a battery of professional experts. Here is a curious paradox: desire for respect from the rest of the academy, accompanied by what amounts to devaluation of the traditional academic disciplines. Historically, polemics often accompany the growth of a new discipline—one thinks, for instance, of psychology's anxiety of influence about its forebear, philosophy. This is the nature of carving out new intellectual turf. But some leadership advocates, among them Joseph Rost and John Gardner, go further. They distrust the knowledge-building enterprise of the university itself. Unlike James MacGregor Burns, the single most influential figure in academic leadership studies, Rost and Gardner do not comfortably wear the mantle of scholarship. Gardner's major claim to authority is based on his service as HEW Secretary in the Johnson Administration. Rost, who directs this country's only Ph.D. program in leadership at the

University of San Diego, stresses in his book *Leadership for the Twenty-First Century* the role of the "scholar-practitioner."

A close reading of that hyphenated term suggests that scholarship isn't enough to satisfy anyone with a true appetite for leading, and that scholarship by itself cannot constitute a full-fledged "practice." At the same time, the hyphenated term implicitly announces that the emerging discipline transcends the academy precisely because it is more than mere scholarship; it is scholarship *plus*. In other words, the new discipline is more practical, or in the vernacular of the sixties, of greater "relevance."

Scholars in the field who look to Rost and Gardner face a cruel dilemma: Can you affirm the value of the disciplines in the academy while simultaneously articulating values that denigrate academic activity? The disclaimer comes that experience is not meant to supplant but rather to supplement what happens in the classroom. And of course such an appeal has a perfectly sound pedigree within higher education. Practica appended to, or accompanying, specific degree programs are nothing new or extraordinary. Undergraduates in disciplines such as political science or social work, graduate students in medicine or the humanities, have long been expected to do some work in their field whether that means serving as a congressional intern, working in a child protective services agency, seeing patients in the emergency room, or teaching students in the classroom. Leadership programs have borrowed from this tradition and at least given lip service both to learning theory and to putting that theory into practice. Yet what disturbs me most about conversations with some leadership-program students at my institution is the frequent litany about academic learning being inadequate compared to the "real world" experience of "hands-on" learning. Apt to draw a blank when I inquire who is laying hands on whom, and under what conditions, these young proponents of experiential education usually reply: "Education has to be more than just reading books." It's striking that such pedagogical theory, which makes the short-term sledding easier while selling students short in the long term, can flourish in an age when both academics and business managers agree that moving and manipulating information—that is to say, high levels of textual literacy—*begin to constitute not the means by which workers do their work, but in fact the major work itself.* Precisely in an age when high-level critical thinking and academic skills are more important than ever for directing tasks, planning strategically, achieving, and, yes, even leading, the rhetoric of experiential "hands-on" education, so crucial in the leadership oeuvre, corrodes that understanding.

It should come as no surprise that such rhetoric proves most attractive to students and teachers averse to the rigors of scholarly activity. I would argue, however, that for leadership programs to fulfill their often hyperbolic claims, what is needed is more and better scholarship, not less, and higher standards of textual proficiency rather than more community-volunteer hours. Only by embracing a forum of rigorous intellectual debate will leadership studies ultimately gain the disciplinary legitimacy that scholars like Joseph Rost, particularly, seek.

By the same token, scholarly values hold the promise of preserving leadership studies as a viable field of inquiry once the grant money runs out. Benjamin DeMott's criticism of leadership studies as a recent variety of "academic pork" (*Harper's*, December 1993) must be taken seriously by those of us who teach it. For if the leadership "pork" is to have any enduring shelf life, if it is to avoid the fate of becoming one more academic fad, that endurance will only accrue through sober and rigorous scholarship that seeks to create a lasting body of work—in short, a canon—and through empirical forms of assessment that demonstrate unequivocally that students in leadership programs indeed perform in ways superior to their peers at liberal arts colleges which lack such leadership programs.

Solid scholarship in leadership studies must be independent, including the expertise of academicians and writers in a variety of disciplines. Most important, to attain disciplinary status, such scholarship by definition must subject itself to the scrutiny of those scholars who possess no vested interest in preserving the discipline; indeed those scholars whose most important role is that of debunking the claims of enthusiasts.

The anti-academic rhetoric we find in Rost and Gardner, I argue, is not a new development, but is instead one more manifestation of what Richard Hofstadter described over thirty years ago in *Anti-Intellectualism in American Life* (1964). There he observed, in a chapter titled "Business and Intellect," that

> The anti-intellectualism of businessmen, interpreted narrowly as hostility to intellectuals, is mainly a political phenomenon. But interpreted more broadly as a suspicion of intellect itself, it is part of the extensive American devotion to practicality and direct experience which ramifies through almost every area of American life. With some variations of details suitable to social classes and historical circumstances, the excessive practical bias so often attributed only to business is found almost everywhere in America. . . . Practical vigor is a virtue; what has been spiritually crippling in our history is the tendency to make a mystique of practicality. (236-237)

The title of the chapter is more than a little misleading, because Hofstadter goes on to point out that the Left in America has proven itself just as guilty of this tendency as the Conservative Right. "We need not be surprised," he says, "to find a 'radical' labor reformer like Henry George advising his son that since college would fill his head with things which would have to be unlearned, he should go directly into newspaper work to put himself in touch with the practical world: the same advice might have come from a business tycoon" (237). It is worth remembering that in our recent past, brilliantly anticipated by Hofstadter, the smearing of "pointy-headed" intellectuals was the pastime not only of George Wallace and other Rightists, but also of a New Left which in the Sixties made the shutting down of university classrooms its most famous symbolic gesture. Impatient with a cerebral socialist old guard, the New Left wanted action, and relevance, and action and relevance right away.[3]

Closely related to the dominant tone of anti-intellectualism that ripples through much of the leadership movement is the frequent appeal within its body of literature to social and political analysis which I will call, for lack of better words, illiberal, or antiliberal. Leadership scholars seldom spell out their ideological predispositions, although the tendency is toward communitarian forms of thinking which on the face of things seem to transcend the old Left-Right dichotomy in political life because they plug into a moral vocabulary that sounds unarguably beneficent.

There are several indicators of this propensity by leadership scholars to imbibe communitarian dogma. Most prominent is the frequently-sounded attack on the evils of atomized liberal individualism. Individualism, as Robert Bellah's *Habits of the Heart* (1985) repeatedly emphasizes—beginning with his subtitle—is an obstacle to "commitment." Individualism, in the communitarian usage, always carries a negative charge. Interesting hedging occurs about the language of individual rights; in fact, in many communitarian schemes, individual rights are rather easily dispensed with. The journal edited by leading communitarian Amitai Etzioni, *The Responsive Community*, has at various times suggested "mandatory public service for students and welfare recipients, restrictions on divorce, programs to trace the sexual contacts of HIV-positive people" (Spayde et al., 63). In my estimation it seems all too evident that such agendas rather easily shade into authoritarianism; and the old question of where community ends and conformity begins must be raised with renewed urgency. Within communitarian circles, the stress on obligations, service, and sacrificing for the common good finds repeated and I think lopsided emphasis.

Leadership scholars don't often identify themselves as communitarians. But the attraction is evident, judging by the vocabulary in many leadership programs extolling the virtues of group cooperation, trust, service, "servant leadership," and community. These terms carry the promise of compassion and sensitivity, values that many undergraduates, particularly the youngest students, will find irresistible and impossible to contest. In most leadership programs much less gets said about the importance of skeptical inquiry. Leadership scholar Barbara Kellerman gives a representative indication of how the communitarian agenda has shaped leadership theory in this account of what's ailing American political culture. Highly indebted to Gardner's concept of the American tilt in the direction of "anti-leadership" values, she argues,

> To paint the backdrop of the political context for leadership in America even more vividly let me make two additional points. First, the anti-authority thrust which evolved rather quickly into an anti-leadership political culture was sharpened by the overall ideology that characterized political thinking in America. It has been referred to by Samuel Huntington as the American creed. Consider the key components of

this creed: individualism, egalitarianism, democracy, freedom—not one of these ideals is conducive to followership. Not one of them is sympathetic to the conception of leadership. In fact, one might reasonably claim that the very . . . ideals of individualism, egalitarianism, democracy, and freedom create suspicion of those who seek to be authoritative, to wield power, to exercise influence. (5, 6)

For Kellerman, as for many other leadership scholars, the prime importance of the "leadership" and "followership" dyad is affirmed wholesale, without much inquiry into whether such terminology even begins to summarize the activities of an active, participating citizenry. I, for one, don't think it does. And it *certainly* doesn't speak accurately to the primary activities carried out in the liberal arts classroom. Derived from Burns's seminal 1978 tome *Leadership*, the very terminology of the dyad is reductionist; in spite of the nuances with which Burns attempts to load it, it finally rings out as a peremptory linguistic pair of terms that leaves precious little room for the kind of skeptical Enlightenment achievement of thinkers such as Jefferson. It is a pair of terms of far greater descriptive value for military leadership than for the much more complex workings of a free, democratic society. Further on in the same article, Kellerman wonders in dismay "how our political context . . . is painted (tainted?) by an anti-authority brush" (7).

Kellerman worries that the revolutionary American premium put on "individualism, egalitarianism, democracy, and freedom" will not make for good leaders and followers. The possibility of pluralism, of splintered interests—in sum, of individualism—is simply too hot a package to handle. Yet if she stops short of announcing communitarianism as the elixir that will tame this anarchic brew, other leadership scholars make it very clear. Yoking the communitarian label to the interests of economic national efficiency, Michael Ellerbrock contends that "Individualistic" and "Communitarian" economic models radically differ, and he has no doubts as to which model will prevail. The terms are used as ciphers for the undesirable and desirable characteristics, respectively, in the new economic world order:

The actualized real world differences between communitarian and individualistic capitalism are generally matters of degree; yet, in principle, they reflect contrasting philosophies. . . . Regarding *Humanity*, the communitarian view sees work as a gratifying end in itself, whereas the individualistic view focuses on people as consumers. In terms of *Partnership*, the communitarian view trusts collaboration among labor, management, directors, and government, whereas the individualistic view places its faith in an adversarial system of checks and balances. Regarding *Choice*, the communitarian view patiently focuses on long term profits, whereas the individualistic view pragmatically operates in the here and now. In terms of *Entrepreneurship*, the communitarian view replaces the adage of "Necessity is the mother of invention" with "Happiness [job stability and contentment] is the mother of invention," whereas the individualist view correlates employee creativity with the desire for higher wages. (53)

It has by now become a cliche of current leadership studies to throw out the notion of the Great Man Theory of Leadership (the individual being by definition a category of suspicion) and to substitute it with vaguely beneficent notions of group dynamics. Hierarchy is out, loosely-coupled organic networks are in. On the face of it, this decentered, non-hierarchical vision of leadership—a warm fuzzy that empties "leadership" of all its hard, hierarchical, and lordly overtones—appears quite compatible with radical poststructuralist and deconstructionist theories which also aim to undo the oppressive hierarchies of Western tradition. And it is worth noting that communitarianism's most frequently-invoked enemy—liberal individualism—likewise serves as a favorite whipping-boy in poststructuralist critical theory. Thus by association, at least to the uninitiated, the impression sticks that communitarianism is a progressive and not a conservative ideological movement.

But the communitarian orientation of most leadership scholars is more in line with classical conservative thinking than with any postmodern theory. Undergirding the communitarian litany about social disintegration, which Derek Phillips has comprehensively documented in his book, *Looking Backward: A Critical Appraisal of Communitarian Thought* (1993), is the nostalgist impulse to believe that once upon a time, somewhere, greater social harmony and unity existed, a time and place from which we have fallen away. This habit of invoking a once-good or better society, the moral heights from which we've ignominiously tumbled, is the most striking feature of conservative, and not liberal, political theory, as Karl Mannheim explained over fifty years ago in *Ideology and Utopia*. Traditionally, liberal idealism, like its nineteenth-century competitor, Marxism, invokes a metanarrative of historical progress with the future as its inspiration; by contrast, conservatives tend to find their locus of hope in the recuperation or emulation of a more righteous past.

Leading communitarian theorists, appealing to the notion of "communities of memory," share this conservative impulse to locate in the past a community of virtue. For Alasdair MacIntyre, the model community embodying harmony, justice, and virtue is usually classical Athens; for Robert Bellah, heavily reliant on de Tocqueville's account of late-eighteenth-century American society, the early American republic was such a community of restraint and community. But that notion of the lost, harmonious "we" is precisely the "we" that liberal critics such as Stephen Holmes and Derek Phillips incisively criticize. Careful examination of the actual historical models upon which the virtuous communities of communitarian fantasy are predicated makes it apparent that the virtue was neither ever so universal, nor even so virtuous as we have been led to believe. How inclusive was the harmonious "we" of classical Athens, or the early American republic, or as is most often the case in the writing of John Gardner (heavily reliant on a communitarian schema), the implicit "we" of pre-1960s America, America before it crashed and burned in the flames of Vietnam, race riots, drugs, and rock-and-roll? Who exactly was included in this harmonious "we"? Minorities, women, and gay people may view this social harmony, and social history, with a more jaundiced perspective.

The antiliberalism of current leadership doctrine is not surprising given the emphasis on "common good" arguments that almost always represent individual rights and freedoms as complicit in the fragmentation and fraying of the once-mighty republic. For many students, it is a short leap from Robert Bellah's critique of the cult of individual personal fulfillment in America to a more generalized notion that personal, individual freedoms and rights are in and of themselves forms of narrow self-interest, that is to say, selfishness. In teaching a course on "Theories of Power and Leadership in Narrative" to students minoring in leadership at Marietta College in 1994, I discovered that this was the conclusion some had reached after imbibing the "servant leadership" vocabulary popularized by Robert Greenleaf. There is much that is morally worthy, and even noble, in such affirmations. (The communitarianism of Bellah, with its deep reliance on biblical categories of thinking, may even induce the restoration of anachronistic concepts such as sin and guilt, concepts that of late have appeared on the cusp of popular rediscovery. I should be quick to point out, as well, that it is not only neoconservatives in Gertrude Himmelfarb's salon who seem willing to entertain the possibility that these concepts possess morally salutary value.) Yet what worries me is that unbalanced by a commitment to democratic principles of individual rights, such teaching may all too quickly degenerate into a form of coercive authoritarianism that polices itself under the mantle of self-sacrificing "virtue."[4]

How can we arrive at legitimate notions of the "common good" in a pluralistic community of divergent interests? That's a question most communitarians prefer to beg because the very existence of noisy, divergent individual and group demands usually constitute for them a symptom of liberal dysfunction and fragmentation. While communitarians claim to bring back into balance the notions of individual "rights" and "obligations"—which selfish liberals have ostensibly allowed to slip all out of proportion—they identify the language of rights and individualism in habitually negative terms, linking up with a conservative vocabulary of cultural decline and moral entropy. Parallel to my argument that leadership studies must recuperate a strong sense of academic rigor in order to be a self-sustaining field of inquiry, I would suggest leadership studies must also scrutinize its predisposition toward communitarian forms of thinking. Welcoming liberal, libertarian, and other individualist thinkers into the tent will open the canon of our inquiry, engaging a host of new questions. Some of these questions communitarians will no doubt find uncomfortable. But these questions might spell the difference between a moribund and predictable set of formulas, and a vital, interesting field of inquiry.

2. The New Discipline

The downgrading of the scholarly disciplines of the liberal arts—as somehow constituting limitations or "blinders" to knowledge—is a strategy by which leadership studies can carve out a niche for itself in the academy. In one intriguing version of this argument, Mark Bagshaw claims the need to rejuvenate an ailing liberal arts curriculum through the administering of the leadership booster-shot. Ostensibly to save the liberal arts curriculum, he first declares it near death. Yet he drastically overstates the degree of the illness. "At one time, the liberal arts were the principal method by which educated people understood and engaged the world," Bagshaw writes. "For a number of reasons, the liberal arts lost their social utility and became marginalized," and "their relevance to everyman's everyday life was not apparent, and they were not valued by most people." Enter here, then, leadership studies, tailored "to restore the liberal arts to a central societal role" (93, 99). Bagshaw's grasp of the historical evolution of the classical liberal arts curriculum is superb. Yet it's a remarkable claim, and I think an unsupported one, to suggest that "liberal arts" are now perceived as having little social utility and are therefore "marginal."

If this is the case, then how do we explain the continuing market demand for the B.A. diploma? Indeed, how do we explain the *highest* market demand for B.A.'s minted at private liberal arts colleges that in most instances do not have "leadership" programs whatsoever—and which continue to stress the core disciplines of the arts, sciences, and humanities? If liberal arts are indeed headed for marginality, then it is difficult to explain the 28 percent growth in B.A.'s granted between 1970 and 1989, driven, Louis Menand suggests, by the realization that attainment of a high-paying profession requires a professional degree, which almost always entails prior earning of the prerequisite B.A. And the marketplace would indicate that the bachelor's comes, preferably, from one of the elite liberal arts institutions. If the liberal arts have become marginalized, it's difficult indeed to explain why institutions that emphasize their liberal arts identity seem to garner the greatest prestige in the academic marketplace.

But Bagshaw's argument that much of higher education is irrelevant to real world concerns, and badly in need of reform, fits into a larger history of polemic. To contend that on the whole the academy no longer speaks to "practicality," because learning has become splintered by disciplinary interests,[5] is an impulse with a long pedigree.

As mentioned earlier, particularly Rost's writing can be understood in the context described by Hofstadter's *Anti-Intellectualism in American Life* (1964). Rost makes sympathetic noises about the necessity for leadership studies being properly "interdisciplinary," but a look past the rhetoric reveals quite another attitude: one more properly understood as patently *antidisciplinary*. When a writer claims, as Rost does, that Plato and Nietzsche never wrote about leadership, we must recognize the attempt to do some academic empire-building of one's own. The desire to carve out a niche for leadership studies in the academy as a unique discipline in its own right requires, first, a diagnosis of the academy's brokenness that makes use of one's available splint not optional, but necessary. Concurrently, the development of a specialized jargon or vocabulary accompanies the quest for legitimacy in the academic marketplace, enabling such legitimacy by conferring on the new "discipline" uniqueness. This process of self-legitimation is nowhere so evident as in the work of Rost.

In his reply to three articles in a recent issue of *Wilson Quarterly* (Summer 1994)—one of which was Jacob Heilbrunn's "Can Leadership Be Studied?," included in this volume—Rost wrote:

> The question . . .'Can Leadership Be Studied?'—is rather silly. . . . The answer is: Of course, leadership can be studied. The question should be: Has leadership been studied well (or effectively)? Have the 3,000 books and articles on leadership, mentioned in your introduction to the articles, helped scholars and practitioners understand leadership better than what common sense would tell us? Have they made a difference in our political and organizational lives, in a good life that we all want to live? (155)

Rost seems to suggest that no one before him has usefully addressed questions of leadership. Attacking Alan Ryan's discussion of classic texts and leadership, he cavalierly dismisses with one phrase two and a half millennia of Western intellectual tradition: "The extended discussions of Plato, Aristotle, Machiavelli, and Weber are beside the point, as none of them wrote about leadership." With the case thus closed on the classical, he dispenses with even more brio the voices of the twentieth century: "The realities of the sad state of leadership studies for the last 75 years are painstakingly documented in my book."

Such stuff is enough to make Newt Gingrich's twenty hours of Empowerment Network history lessons look like real beef. Even so, Rost sometimes verges on interesting questions in his book *Leadership for the Twenty-First Century* (1991), which James MacGregor Burns claims may be the "Bible" of the leadership-by-consensus school (xii).

For one thing, Rost accurately evaluates the current state of leadership studies as overwhelmingly dominated by the paradigms of social psychology and business management. He asks why other disciplines' narratives of leadership have been ignored, those of "anthropological, historical, political, and sociological" orientation (29). It's a good point; Weber may, after all, be worthy of consideration. Oddly left out of this list, however, are art and literature, which more often than not are exactly about cultural constructions of leadership and power. Even stranger an omission, though, is economics, especially noteworthy when we consider that the overall thesis of Rost's book is the by-now familiar line taken by everyone from Robert Reich to Alvin Toffler that the economy is shifting from the old industrial base to one of newer information technologies. Rost's unique signature on this boilerplate is that the industrial economy was driven by hierarchically-structured "managers" while the new "postindustrial" style of leadership will be epitomized by leaders—not managers—who utilize non-coercive consensus models of interaction.

Rost argues at his book's outset that leadership studies must of necessity be interdisciplinary (16), yet he has shown, since the book's publication, a remarkably crude attitude more suggestive of antidisciplinary than interdisciplinary enthusiasm. In this respect Rost reiterates platitudes first articulated by an older "expert" in leadership studies, John Gardner. Gardner, perhaps best-known for his 1990 work *On Leadership*, struck a pose early in his career against academe. In *No Easy Victories*

(1968), Gardener argues that leadership properly understood does not draw on the resources of professional expertise or academic professionalism, but in fact must stand against such academic values:

> We are immunizing a high proportion of our most gifted young people against any tendencies to leadership. . . . Most of our intellectually gifted young people go from college directly into graduate school or into one of the older and more prestigious professional schools. There they are introduced to—or, more correctly, powerfully indoctrinated in—a set of attitudes appropriate to scholars, scientists, and professional men. This is all to the good. The students learn to identify themselves strongly with their calling and its ideals. They acquire a conception of what a good scholar, scientist or professional man is like. As things stand now, however, that conception leaves little room for leadership in the normal sense; the only kind of leadership encouraged is that which follows from the performing of purely professional tasks in a superior manner. Entry into what most of us would regard as the leadership roles in the society at large is discouraged. In the early stages of a career there is a good reason for this: becoming a first-class scholar, scientist or professional requires single-minded dedication. Unfortunately, by the time the individual is sufficiently far along in this career to afford a broadening of interest, he often finds himself irrevocably set in a narrow mold. (127–129)

The necessary progress of the successful "leader," then, according to Gardner, is fulfilled by nothing less than the dismissal of academic or professional specialization and the joining of the ranks of gentlemen amateurs who know better. And the singular ignominy of staying in the academy, according to him, is to suffer "the leadership vaccine": "It is not that professors propound these views and students learn them. Rather, they are in the air and students absorb them" (129). Higher education, in this view, becomes toxic. Too much time spent in the academy will result in the kind of specialization which, according to Gardner, destroys one's ability to lead. Rost, like Gardner, seems suspicious of too much learning, ultimately making an argument that attempts to transcend rather than master the disciplines.

A similar form of hubris carries over into Rost's analysis of recent scholarship in the field of leadership studies. Dismissing Great Man theories of leadership as well as attributes theories, Rost goes on to make the grand pronouncement of his book, namely, that Leaders (postindustrial non-coercive visionaries) by definition cannot be Managers (industrial hierarchical dinosaurs). But this dualistic schema is hardly original; it simply retreads James MacGregor Burns's more academic distinction between exciting Transformational leaders and the boring Transactional kind.

Rost seems well aware that shouting the word "leadership" from every housetop is hardly an answer for thinking people: "Leadership scholars need to get rid of the notion that leadership is the answer to all of our group, organizational, and societal problems. People who lead often do the wrong things in their attempt to solve problems" (77). But Rost's definition of leadership, one of mutual goals sought out by consensus within the body politic, seemingly attained without any conflict, force, or coerciveness whatsoever (102), discourages study of realpolitik that falls short of this Rogerian utopianism. Thus his model of leadership ultimately makes discussion of the "wrong things" done in the name of leadership beside the point. It's a curious paradox.

This refusal to engage the potential dark side of the leadership impulse—or else simplistic gesture of dumping that entire dark side in the lap of industrial-hierarchical "managers"—ultimately reveals the Dale Carnegie fabric of Rost's book. This becomes apparent in his oft-trumpeted definition of leadership itself: "Leadership is an influence relationship among leaders and followers who intend real changes that reflect their mutual purposes" (102). The definition is fascinating in that Rost attempts to blunt the conflictual edge of what is essentially a dyadic command-obedience model in Burns's terminology of "leadership" and "followership"—terminology which, not surprisingly, infuses the Marine Corps training manual. As a rhetorical move, the phrase "mutual purposes" is meant to overcome the same inherent tension. But what happens when "mutual purposes" are not discovered? Rost's argument that "morally purposeful action" (87) by definition excludes "coercive" activity of any kind certainly helps keep leadership's hands clean, but his theorizing, I would reemphasize, seems very far removed indeed from the world of decisions that prime ministers, presidents, college deans, and even parish ministers must often make. As students, teachers, or "practitioners," we are finally left by Rost to the activity of applauding a repetitive series of utopian moral affirmations. I would contend, however, that it's difficult if not impossible to build a curriculum on this model.

Defining what exactly "morally purposeful action" (87) is might conceivably move us off the dime. But Rost doesn't ever get around to explaining it, or how individuals or groups might determine this moral purposefulness. Perhaps leaders and followers who are in perfect synchronicity by Rost's model intuitively know of what that moral purposefulness consists. One looks in vain for the briefest discussion of how different cultures, religions, or philosophical schools might interpret "morally purposeful action," or of the criteria needed to evaluate this moral purposefulness. Most crucially, that a group of people can work in perfect harmony and mutual purposefulness toward horrific ends seems to me a possibility that Rost's definition does not even address.

Leadership studies must take up all these questions. But it is as yet unestablished that the new "discipline" Rost speaks for can substantially improve or enlarge on what traditional liberal arts disciplines of the social sciences, literature, religion, or moral philosophy already have to offer in this regard.

Carving out his new academic turf, Rost reiterates his own definition of leadership with white-knuckled insistence throughout his book. But his definition is finally ethically vacuous. "Leadership is an influence relationship among leaders and followers who intend real changes that reflect their mutual purposes" (102). What Rost means by "real change" is the biggest question begged. It would seem to connect with our evolution from Dark Age Managers to New Age Leaders in the exciting world of the technological, knowledge-based economy. But the Rostofarian take on economic history reveals itself as rosy-hued, even a little naive. Does Rost realize that this New Age humanist vocabulary of care and consensus is exactly that used by numerous corporate "downsizing" and "reengineering" consultants in the 1980s and 1990s? Eventually Rost's narrative, burdened by jargon and contradiction, reaches a critical mass of incoherence. Disputing leadership that relies on or asks for outcomes orientation—because that is anachronistically "industrial"—Rost insists that the "intention" of real changes is more important than "outcomes." By this point whatever argument Rost was making has been lost, and his use of the phrase "real change" is as empty as his use of the concept "morally purposeful." A little Plato could go a long way. Maybe even some Augustine, Locke, or John Stuart Mill. But then, Rost proposes that Plato never spoke to the subject.

3. The Communitarian Prescription

The idea that leadership studies can provide one avenue of restoring America's fraying values is central to the service-learning movement which has roots in JFK's "Ask not what your country can do for you" speech, as well as George Bush's "Thousand Points of Light," and which has continued most recently in Bill Clinton's Americorps program. At the level of ideas, the intertwined theme of leadership and service defines in a central way the communitarian theory of the state. And it is to their credit that leading communitarians—among them most prominently Amitai Etzioni, Robert Bellah, and Alasdair MacIntyre—seem more willing, or maybe it is more conscious, than Rost and Gardner to acknowledge the intellectual tradition that guides their idea of moral purpose.

Uncritically affirmed communitarianism, however, is problematic too, and as a core ideology in leadership studies it holds, as I have already suggested, the potential to obfuscate issues vital to a democratic society. The most searching questions about communitarian thought have emerged from a renewed liberal intellectual tradition which, until 1989, theorists of both conservative and Marxist persuasion had largely written off as doddering or dead. Before reviewing some of these questions, it's worth speaking more fully about the communitarian prescription to the ills it diagnoses.

If communitarians usually hold up individualism and consumerism as the villains destroying Western civilization, their response is healthy doses of social service or voluntarism, a return to community and solidarity. But it is precisely in this desire to impose, by way of mandated forms of "community" or service, that communitarianism reveals its most antiliberal features. The more we consider the literature of communitarian thought, or the public pronouncements of its advocates, the more disturbing the implications become.

The first major problem with communitarian doctrine is that its propensity to idealize past communities of virtue usually requires the use of warped historical lenses. Derek Phillips observes in *Looking Backward* that the communities of memory invoked by communitarian spokesmen seldom resemble the actual historical communities upon which they are ostensibly based, whether we speak of ancient Athens or pre-1960s America (chapters two and six). The mythologizing, nostalgist nature of this impulse to enshrine some past community is connected to communitarians' own overt affirmation of the religious dimension of human life: they are fond of affirming some kind of spirituality, however fuzzy, which they hold up in contrast to the spiritual vacuum they perceive at the heart of Enlightenment liberal theory.

The fall from virtue, according to most communitarian analysts, has mostly to do with atomistic individualism, a disease which translates into disrespect for authority, or just plain bad attitude. Rost's diatribe against "cultural permissiveness" (17), Kellerman's handwringing about the "anti-authority attitude," and Warren Bennis's assertion that "An unconscious conspiracy in contemporary society prevents leaders . . . from taking charge and making changes" (xii) all share a longing for a time when proper respect for authority reigned. I would submit this is the center of most communitarian thought. John Gardner, to whom these writers seem indebted, first began to expostulate against the social disintegration he saw around him in the late 1960s. The railing strongly anticipated communitarian rhetoric. Gardner's writings consistently indicate a desire for the center to still hold, for a time when the fragmentation of wayward individual desire was still maintained in check by the social bond. It is the classic communitarian line, implying the existence of a better past from which we've strayed. As he says in *On Leadership*:

> A great many of our contemporaries, left without moorings by the disintegration of group norms and torn from any context of shared obligations, have gotten drunk on self. We value the individual. We value individuality. . . . But we cannot respect the crazy celebration of self that one sees today. Intellectuals of the 1960s cried 'Life is absurd'. . . . (114)

In 1970, when the youth were disturbing the peace because of Vietnam—but about which he is remarkably silent—Gardner took to ranting:

> Accompanying the hostility to established institutions is a breakdown in authority, in just about every dimension: the authority of parents, religion, custom, social class, the law, and the state. Not only has authority been eroded; critics have developed extraordinarily effective techniques for cutting public figures down to size. The politics of derision turns out to be devastatingly effective, and—in an unhealthy way—downright fun. No one who has reviewed the sweep of American history will believe that our leaders and public figures—at every level of public life—are any more deficient in quality than they were a decade or a century ago. That they seem so is due partly to the breakdown in authority and partly to our increased skill of stripping them of dignity. Men in power have never been fully protected by the mantle of respect surrounding high office, but today they are naked as jaybirds. (Gardner 1970, 30-31)

As Derek Phillips points out, communitarianism shares with certain strains of conservative and authoritarian ideology a deep belief in an idealized past dispensation. Phillips argues that the most serious problem with communitarian ideology is its distortion of history. In examining the societies to which communitarian critics often return in their imaginations for moral solace, Phillips suggests their advocates need to reconsider some of the central features of these harmonious, organic societies. Misogyny, slavery, ethnocentrism—these are only a few of the features Phillips argues the communitarians want to overlook, or at least underplay. And just as importantly, Phillips points out that the "unified" cultural values which these earlier communities allegedly embodied were indeed values "shared"—by small elites consisting almost always of privileged white males.

Closely allied to the communitarian diagnosis that an emphasis on individual rights has ballooned to a dangerous point is the glib facility with the phrase, "the common good," and the related notion of the necessity of noble sacrifice for a larger cause. Might not there be a variety of ways or variety of communities expressing their respective notions of the common good? Might not "the common good" take us back, in its darkest moments, to forms of majoritarian tyranny? Might not the notion of sacrifice be, more often than not, the patriotic gilding used to justify the waste of human life in ill-conceived wars? In other words, might not sacrifice for the common good need equal measures of serious reappraisal as well as affirmation for its potential to ennoble human life? All these questions must be raised. That they are not usually raised by communitarians should give us pause, especially if communitarian ideology becomes the font at which students in leadership studies drink, to the exclusion of all other fonts. The notion of "the common good" is indeed an urgent one. But I want my students to affirm it only insofar as they recognize two closely related issues: (1) We must recognize that historically the two most prominent causes identified with "the common good" have been religious orthodoxy, and loyalty to the state, as Holmes points out in "The Permanent Structure of Antiliberal Thought." With troubling regularity, nationalism and fundamentalism have emphatically invoked the language of sacrifice for a common cause. (2) If we talk of achieving the common good then we must be willing to identify, as John Rawls would have us do, the particular individual(s), class(es), or group(s) not likely to share in any particular version of "the common good" we decide to implement.

A liberal and skeptical position on leadership must put under scrutiny any kind of ideological formation that presents false dichotomies. Unfortunately, communitarian analyses lend themselves all too often to forms of intellectual dualism. The emphasis within current leadership theory on "the common good" vis-a-vis forms of atomistic individualism simply confirms Holmes's contention that communitarians are typically fond of "simplifying dichotomies, notably to the contrasts of private interest versus public virtue and base individualism versus noble community." Holmes argues that "these alternatives are unsatisfactory, first of all, because they obscure the possibility of private virtue. They also suggest that individualism is necessarily antisocial" (233).

False dichotomies abound in leadership studies, as in many demagogic movements. James MacGregor Burns's touchstone book *Leadership* (1978) offers with its labels of "transformational" and "transactional" leadership facile tools for many undergraduates to oversimplify the political and social complications of their world. Like the arcane terminology of any new discourse, the jargon was bound for certain abuse. I recall one student's insistence that these impressive multisyllabics could exhaustively account for the differences between Moses and Joshua.

Yet most problematic of all the dichotomies that mark contemporary leadership theory is the coinage "leadership-followership," or "leader/follower," also derived from Burns's work, terms whose usage I have yet to fully comprehend. Do these terms denote two separate activities, or forms of life? Do they describe a simultaneous or an alternating mutuality, one organic and yet "loosely-coupled"? Do they suggest leaders actually follow, and/or vice versa?

Most objectionable about the language of Burns is its limiting of the imagination, of the possibilities for action which may not be well described by either "leading" or "following," by certain forms of dissent and formulation of alternative strategies that are not encompassed by any of these terms. There exist multiple forms of public discourse, or even strategic forms of inaction, silence, and even strategies of intentional disobedience that group members and sometimes outsiders can embrace in their participation in the life of a democratic republic.

Most emphatically, however, I find Burns's vocabulary inadequate because it elides the most important work we do in a democratic society: skeptical inquiry, critical thinking, creative problem-solving. These are activities which begin by identifying important issues and the public agenda—not by asking how one fits into anyone's schema of "leading" or "following." Recalling Kellerman's words, however, about the American experiment, it seems precisely on grounds of alternative possibility, of creative dissent within organizations that eludes facile categorization of either leading or following per se, that much leadership theory in its present mode exhibits its most antiliberal tendencies: "Consider the key components of this creed: individualism, egalitarianism, democracy, freedom—not one of these ideals is conducive to followership. Not one of them is sympathetic to the conception of leadership."

She is right. What Kellerman seems unwilling to entertain is the possibility that the dyad not only lifts to primary status what is of secondary importance, but also distorts what is profoundly new and desirable about the American experiment. I would submit that we may find better terminologies that describe what democracy does, and the way it works. Indeed, the American experiment was predicated on a suspicion of both leadership and followership as forms of life lived out in the aristocratic arrangements of the Old World. Leadership theory following Burns's dualistic terminology limits itself essentially to questions of how one fits into the dichotomous model. The new kind of leadership theory I am calling for will question the very premises of that model and seek to supplant it with a more supple and variegated account of existential possibilities for living in the world.

In some quarters, the affirmation of "citizenship," sometimes preceded with the adjectives "critical" or "responsible," has emerged as a comprehensive term meant to supplement the terminology of leading and following in Burns's schema. The connotative element of this term at least accommodates the activity of thinking, as well as the concrete image of walking patrol in a rice paddy (literally leading or following), an image that the leadership-followership dyad almost inevitably invites. But the affirmative language of citizenship itself does not, in my estimation, speak either very well or very exhaustively for the task of helping form liberally-educated human beings, a task which involves scrutiny of every shibboleth, even the patriotic ones. "Being a good citizen is not the same thing as being wise, unbiased, humane, or unusually independent," Judith Shklar writes in *The Faces of Injustice*. "Rousseau was on solid ground when he noted that the best citizens were xenophobic and bellicose."[6]

4. The Study of Leadership in a Time of New Tribalism

The Marine Corps training manual (1984) contains an illuminating passage for aiding leaders faced with the likely question to come from new inductees who have imbibed the American passion for inquiry and dissent: "IS IT DISLOYAL TO DISAGREE WITH LEADERS OR DO WE HAVE A RESPONSIBILITY TO DO SO?" The scripted response painfully, and unsuccessfully, attempts to merge both a commitment to humanist values as well as to the irrevocable military dyad of leader and follower:

> It is not disloyal to disagree or speak one's piece *at the proper time and place*, provided that we remember our duty to follow orders without question. The leader requires all the input he can get from us to help him make a clear-eyed decision. The "we" not the "they" are the Marine Corps. We must get involved to improve things. (9)

What to liberals is precisely the valuable American habit of vigilance and suspicion toward one's leaders, a habit most eloquently articulated in Sidney Hook's *The Hero in History: A Study in Limitation and Possibility* (1943), usually appears to enthusiasts of leadership studies as stubborn obstructionism or incivility. The responses to political authority posed by liberal and communitarian writers pose a sharp contrast. The temperaments of liberal and communitarian thought are in radical disjunction: they will invoke, respectively, very different intellectual genealogies, as well as ask very different questions in the course of such study.

History in its current phase seems a far more complicated matter to me than the communitarian diagnosticians would make it. Certainly the tribalist and fundamentalist furies after the end of the Cold War would suggest that our problems, both nationally and globally, have as much to do with fanatical groups (leaders and followers working for mutual purposes, and usually full of righteous moral purposefulness) as they do with rampant individualism and materialism. Ironically, notes Stephen Holmes, "The greatest threat to social cohesion . . . arises not from individualism but from collective passions, ideological conflict, and inherited rivalries between hostile factions. In factional settings, solidarity is a problem not a solution" (233).

I would submit that as an educator in the liberal arts tradition, my primary task is to teach students not necessarily how to lead or to follow. Rather, my task is to teach them first and always how to think. Nothing—including the rhetoric of experiential learning, or call of civic responsibility, or the imperative for social and group cohesion—should obscure this central mission. If my task is to help individuals form habits of critical thinking that ultimately enhance freedom and curb injustice, this will necessarily involve learning habits of suspicion as well as trust, confidence in the individual conscience that can offset the worst inclinations of groupthink. Holmes's remarks are vital. As leadership scholars we can ill afford to trade in the traditional liberal arts mandate for an ideological belief that inscribes conformity in the name of community—however morally attractive, or even "progressive," that conformity initially appears.

Notes

1. Any beginning point for a genealogy is necessarily arbitrary. The establishment of the Center for Creative Leadership in Greensboro, NC, in 1970 is one such useful date, since the CCL from its inception has played the role of documenting major programs in leadership in both corporate America and American higher education through such vehicles as the annually published *Leadership Source Book*.

2. The degree to which the military is imbued with the rhetoric of leadership, and has also influenced contemporary study of leadership, should not be underestimated—and needs much more thorough attention than I can give in this brief essay. The prevalence, one might even say the promiscuity with which the word is wielded in this context was brought home with terrible force in Timothy McVeigh's declaration in *Newsweek* magazine: "After I got through the leadership . . . course, I recognized that I could do what needs to be done as a leader" (3 July 1995, 18).

   Leadership has long been a prime military preoccupation. As Bernard Bass observes, the first systematic compilation of leadership literature was begun in 1946 with a grant from the Office of Naval Research (xiv). Equally important, I think, is a continuing pattern of military background and training that is more rather than less common among administrators of high-profile leadership programs. Not coincidentally, the first dean of the Jepson School—site of the nation's only major in leadership studies—established his credentials at West Point. (And maybe not surprisingly, the groundbreaking and inauguration ceremonies at the Jepson School included the ROTC and helicopters.) William E. Rosenbach, who directs the Eisenhower Leadership Program Grant funded by the U.S. Department of Education, is also co-author of *Military Leadership: In Search of Excellence* (2e., Westview Press, 1992). Even those not of military background nonetheless are apt to benchmark their programs against West Point and Annapolis. Steve Schwartz, who directs Marietta College's McDonough Center for Leadership and Business, calls Marietta "America's Leadership College" on the basis of there being "more leadership activities at MC than at any other college or university with the exception of military institutions" (*Marcolian*, 23 February 1995, 1).

3. The enduring criticism about the New Left, made by the older socialist and liberal intellectuals who watched in dismay as the youth barricaded classrooms, addresses this propensity to leap into action without adequate intellectual and analytical tools. My dissertation director, Irving

Howe, used to tell a story that has already become apocryphal: heckled by an antiwar demonstrator for his lack of passion, Howe replied, "You're going to be a dentist." The relationship in America between practical activism—of any political persuasion—and academic contemplation has never been an easy one to negotiate.

4. I am reminded of Leni Riefenstahl's recollection of one of Hitler's most eloquent appeals, one rooted in the vocabulary of compassion, neighborliness, and economic justice:

> He swore to them that he would create a new Germany and put an end to unemployment and poverty. When he said: 'Collective good takes precedence over individual good,' his words struck at my heart. I had always been preoccupied with my personal interests and given little thought to other people. I had lived very egocentrically. I felt ashamed and at this point I felt ready to make the sacrifices he called for. (123)

5. It's worth noting that this kind of rhetoric—that the disciplines **limit** rather than **liberate** understanding—is also part of the intellectual apparatus of much of the poststructuralist avant-garde theory scene. Yet it's also significant to note that such rhetoric can be wielded in disturbing ways. In the case of Bennington College's recent reorganization—which included the elimination of all departments, the firing of tenured faculty, and by most accounts the end of freedom of expression on the campus—the trustees' reorganization "Plan" notably included exactly this rhetoric about instruction that goes beyond disciplinary "confines," and the necessity of "teacher-practitioners."

6. Or, as Stephen Holmes explains in "Liberalism for a World of Ethnic Passions and Decaying States:" "Liberals are not blind to loyalty, therefore, but instead assume that loyalty is sometimes good and sometimes bad, depending largely on the way conflicting affiliations and affinities are handled politically. While liberals are not anticommunitarian in a militant sense, they reasonably refuse to apotheosize loyalty as the source of all meaning and the highest human good, insisting that a sharp distinction be made between group identifications to be encouraged and factionalism and xenophobias to be discouraged. To draw the all-important line between creative and destructive loyalties, liberals usually invoke another set of values, necessarily distinct from loyalty itself—justice, peace, and the mutually enriching and enlivening power of human diversity" (Holmes 1994, 601–602).

Works Cited

Bagshaw, Mark. "Liberating the Liberal Arts Through Leadership Studies: An Essay." *Journal of Leadership Studies* 2 (1995), no. 1: 93–109.

Bass, Bernard M., *Bass and Stogdill's Handbook of Leadership: Theory, Research, and Managerial Application*. 3e. New York: Free Press, 1990.

Bellah, Robert N. et al. *Habits of the Heart: Individualism and Commitment in American Life*. New York: Harper & Row, 1985.

Bennis, Warren G. *Why Leaders Can't Lead: The Unconscious Conspiracy Continues*. San Francisco: Jossey-Bass, 1989.

Burns, James MacGregor. *Leadership*. New York: Harper & Row, 1978.

DeMott, Benjamin. "Choice Academic Pork: Inside the Leadership-Studies Racket." *Harper's* (December 1993): 61–77.

Ellerbrock, Michael. "Education for Economic Leadership: Vision is the Key." *Journal of Leadership Studies* 2 (1995), no. 1: 50–57.

Gardner, John W. *No Easy Victories*. New York: Harper & Row: 1968.

———. *On Leadership*. New York: Free Press, 1990.

———. *The Recovery of Confidence*. New York: W. W. Norton, 1970.

Greenleaf, Robert K. *Servant Leadership*. New York: Paulist, 1977.

Hofstadter, Richard. *Anti-Intellectualism in American Life*. 1964; New York: Vintage, 1966.

Holmes, Stephen. *The Anatomy of Antiliberalism*. Cambridge: Harvard University Press, 1993.

———. "Liberalism for a World of Ethnic Passions and Decaying States." *Social Research* 61 (Fall 1994): 599–610.

———. "The Permanent Structure of Antiliberal Thought." In *Liberalism and the Moral Life*, ed. Nancy R. Rosenblum. Cambridge: Harvard University Press, 1989.

Kellerman, Barbara. "Leadership in the Political Context." *Journal of Leadership Studies* 1 (1994), no. 4: 4–9.

Marine Corps Training Manual. 1984.

Menand, Louis. "What Are Universities For? The Real Crisis on Campus is One of Identity." *Harper's* (December 1991): 47–56.

Phillips, Derek L. *Looking Backward: A Critical Appraisal of Communitarian Thought.* Princeton: Princeton University Press, 1993.

Rawls, John. *A Theory of Justice.* Cambridge: Harvard University Press, 1971.

Riefenstahl, Leni. *A Memoir.* New York: St. Martin's, 1995.

Rosenbach, William E. *Military Leadership: In Search of Excellence.* 2e. New York: Westview, 1992.

Rost, Joseph. *Leadership for the Twenty-First Century.* New York: Praeger, 1991.

———. Letter to the editor. *Wilson Quarterly* 18 (Summer 1994): 155.

Shklar, Judith. *The Faces of Injustice.* Cambridge: Harvard University Press, 1990.

Spayde, Jon et al. "100 Visionaries Who Could Change Your Life." *Utne Reader* (January–February 1995): 54–81.

4

Teaching Leadership/Teaching Ethics: Martin Luther King's "Letter From Birmingham Jail"

Peter S. Temes

The most brutal front-page images from the American Civil Rights Movement—firehoses turned on young African American children, attack dogs urged on by police to sink their teeth into the bodies of peaceful protesters—document life in Birmingham, Alabama, in April and May of 1963. In those months, Martin Luther King Jr. led a series of protests aimed at desegregating the city's downtown retail workforce, its bus stations, and its public eating places. King himself was arrested in Birmingham, and he used his solitude in jail as an opportunity to respond to a group of local religious leaders who had urged him to give up his protests and go back to his home in Atlanta. Bit by bit, King smuggled out of his cell the text that became known as his "Letter From Birmingham Jail."

"I am in Birmingham," King wrote in his letter,

> because injustice is here. Just as the prophets of the eighth century B.C. left their villages and carried their 'Thus saith the Lord' far beyond the boundaries of their home towns, and just as the Apostle Paul left his village of Tarsus and carried the Gospel of Jesus Christ to the far corners of the Greco-Roman world, so I am compelled to carry the gospel of freedom beyond my hometown. (77)

King's effectiveness as a leader is undisputed—at 26, with only the small institutional authority of a newly hired minister in Montgomery, Alabama's second-best church, King helped turn a local bus boycott into a movement that took up the unfinished work of the Civil War and Reconstruction. Yet scholars of leadership have had relatively little to say about King, beyond the obvious work of classifying him as a religious leader, a charismatic figure, and a powerfully effective public speaker.

King, a Christian minister, was motivated by faith. I am not a Christian, yet I find King more convincing than most leaders because he articulated the specific meaning he found in his faith so fully. By this I mean that King did not merely refer to the ideas that drove him, but he explained them in careful detail. His mode of leadership was almost entirely philosophical, and almost entirely impersonal—he made no claims for himself, or for any other man or woman, but demanded attention to ideas. To take King as a model of leadership, then, is to define leadership in an unusual way—not as the action of King as an individual, but as the action of the ideas he brought forth again and again. From reading King, I come to this definition of leadership: Leadership is the action of ideas to make change, through the agency of individuals.

What were the ideas that King brought forward in his "Letter From Birmingham Jail"? These three:

* that good and evil exist, and are always battling each other;
* that peace that suppresses this conflict between good and evil is harmful; and
* that institutional authority, like the authority of laws, is never adequate to distinguish the good from the evil.

Each of these three ideas suggests challenges for the study of leadership.

The first idea, about the existence of good and evil, is in its broadest terms a hotly debated topic at American colleges and universities today. Some scholars propose that good and evil (along with other abstract qualities like artfulness, or masculinity) are entirely relative, created and taught by the complex forces of socialization. "Social Constructivism" is the most common label for this camp, and it clearly opposes the notion that absolute qualities exist in their own right, to be discovered by people rather than created by people. King clearly belongs in the opposite camp, committed to the philosophy generally called "essentialism." In fact, King subtlety implies that his critics are the relativists here, in light of their suggestions that what might look like ugly racism in some other town is actually something else in Birmingham, and that local standards of right and wrong matter most.

"I am cognizant," King responds to that relativism, "of the interrelatedness of all communities and states. I cannot sit idly by in Atlanta and not be concerned with what happens in Birmingham. Injustice anywhere is a threat to justice everywhere" (77). King's essentialism cuts directly against the technique-centered approach to teaching leadership. Being a good leader, from the perspective of King's essentialism, would have little to do with mobilizing groups to action, or with responding to their collective will. Instead, leadership would need to be entirely about advancing the essential good. Strong technique without proper grounding in the good would be utterly worthless.

The clerical critics King's "Letter" nominally addresses are themselves, in King's model, poor leaders. Perhaps their technique is good, certainly their social authority is distinct, and many, indeed a majority, of the citizens of Birmingham were behind these leaders, but they were bad leaders nonetheless, because they were motivated by poor ideas. "You deplore the demonstrations taking place in Birmingham," King writes.

> But your statement, I am sorry to say, fails to express a similar concern for the conditions that brought about the demonstrations. I am sure that none of you would want to rest content with the superficial kind of social analysis that deals merely with effects and does not grapple with underlying causes. It is unfortunate that demonstrations are taking place in Birmingham, but it is more unfortunate that the city's white power structure left the Negro community with no alternative. (77-78)

The city's white power structure included most of the clergy who had written the original letter criticizing King. His principal response to them is to tell them they are wrong, and to caution them to pay less attention to the Civil Rights Movement's tactic—their disruptive demonstrations—and more to the essential rightness of its cause. In my view, this is a lesson that teachers of leadership ought to emphasize constantly. Leadership into the abyss is not properly leadership at all.

King's second principal idea in the "Letter From Birmingham Jail"—the idea that any peace that suppresses the conflict between good and evil is harmful—builds off of King's essentialism. King lays out this second notion directly:

> I had hoped that the white moderate would understand that law and order exist for the purpose of establishing justice and that when they fail in this purpose they become the dangerously structured dams that block the flow of social progress. I had hoped that the white moderate would understand that the present tension in the South is a necessary phase of transition from an obnoxious peace, in which the Negro passively accepted his plight, to a substantive and positive peace, in which all men will respect the dignity and worth of human personality. Actually, we who engage in nonviolent direct action are not the creators of tension. We merely bring to the surface the hidden tension that is already alive. We bring it out in the open, where it can be seen and dealt with. (85)

That action to "bring to the surface the hidden tension that is already alive" is central to effective and just leadership. And that action is entirely dependent on prior social reflection: the leader, before taking action, must seek to understand what tensions do indeed exist, what crises lie in potential below the surface of an inappropriate calm.

This means paying broad and deep attention to the lives of people throughout our society. King could lead because he lived and worked among ordinary people who were oppressed. He could lead because he sought to understand what they wanted and what they needed. No theory about the nature of leadership and no understanding of the traits of leaders in general could substitute for this. To teach students to be leaders, then, we must help them cultivate a serious understanding of ordinary people as they live their lives today. To cultivate qualities of leadership in our students, we must strive to instill in them the habit of social observation, of asking about the lives of everyone who lives and works with them, and for them, above them, below them, and beside them.

Beyond this specific knowledge of the substance of life for those whom he led, King also held a clear idea of what these people deserved. As a Christian, and following in a particular tradition that extends, in this century, back to Walter Rauschenbusch's 1907 book *Christianity and the Social Crisis*,

King could approach his desire to make social change with a deeply held knowledge of what was right and what was wrong in the social structure that he and his followers found themselves within. To extend this from King to leaders in general: Only with a clear idea of what a good society is, what rights each man and woman truly deserves, can the leader begin to take action.

This offers a powerful lesson for college leadership studies: to teach leadership, first we must lead our students to clarify their values about issues like economic and social stratification. Only with a clear sense of their own values can they propose to function as ethical leaders.

This task of defining values is usually ignored by leadership theorists, and only superficially taken up by most leadership teachers. At best, theorists and teachers will talk about "the common good," or—taking Bernard Bass as a notable example—cast the ethical aspects of leadership in ultimately empty terms. Bass writes—paraphrasing James MacGregor Burns—that in following a good leader,[1] "[f]ollowers' attitudes, beliefs, motives, and confidence need to be transformed from a lower to a higher plane of arousal and maturity" (xiii). But what is "arousal" of motive? And is arousal necessarily a good thing? What is maturity of attitude? Is maturity the same as goodness? With Bass, as with the writers and teachers who talk endlessly of the "common good" yet do not specifically define it, we wind up with a tautology of morals.[2] To say that good leadership arouses and matures the inner qualities of followers, or to say that good leadership serves the common good, is really to say nothing more than "good leadership is good." Which is, in fact, to say nothing at all.

In my view, serious contemplation of the nature and the practical qualities of a just society **must** go hand in hand with any efforts to teach about leadership.

King articulates his third notion, that institutional authority is often opposed to the good, specifically in terms of the segregation laws he and his fellow protestors were trying to overturn in Birmingham. He repeats Augustine's distinction between just and unjust laws: "I would be the first to advocate obeying just laws," he writes. "One has not only a legal but a moral responsibility to obey just laws. Conversely, one has a moral obligation to disobey unjust laws" (82). King goes further, offering a reasoned distinction between the two kinds of laws. "An unjust law is a code that a numerical or power majority group compels a minority group to obey but does not make binding on itself. . . . By the same token, a just law is a code that a majority compels a minority to follow and that it is willing to follow itself." And further still, explaining that "sometimes a law is just on its face and unjust in its application. For instance," he continues, "I have been arrested for parading without a permit. Now, there is nothing wrong in having an ordinance which requires a permit for a parade. But such an ordinance becomes unjust when it is used to maintain segregation and to deny citizens the First-Amendment privilege of peaceful assembly and protest."

But to disobey is not to "evade" or "defy" a law, in King's view. "One who breaks an unjust law must do so openly, lovingly, and with a willingness to accept the penalty" (83).

A great body of scholarship takes up the implications of just law theory, and those implications are indeed far-reaching. I'm most interested in the way that King's moral sense brings that debate directly to each of his followers. He asks these people to break the law. He explains, morally, why the law-breaking is necessary. And he then asks them to suffer the consequences of their law-breaking within the larger legal system. He demands remarkable restraint, and remarkable thought on the part of his followers. His respect for their moral and intellectual substance is surprisingly deep.

Why surprisingly? Because King's interest in their moral and intellectual substance transcends any notion of getting them to do what he wants them to do. He *does* want them to do a few things—march, resist the urge to violence, and more—but he wants far more for them to draw closer to good acts and good belief. As a leader, King wanted the ideas he understood to be the truth—ideas about love, human community, and human decency—to make change. But change in the world was hardly his target. The target was vaster: change in the hearts and minds of men and women. James MacGregor Burns describes this kind of leadership as "transforming" in his 1978 book *Leadership*, the most influential theoretical work in the field. "Transforming leadership" happens when "one or more persons *en-*

gage with others in such a way that leaders and followers raise one another to higher levels of motivation and morality" (20). This definition was a vital addition to the study of leadership when Burns first proposed it, and it still resonates. And yet Burns squirms when it comes time for him to talk about just what makes one level of motivation higher than another—he calls in Abraham Maslow and Lawrence Kohlberg, whose definitions of morality were entirely developmental and utterly without the anchoring forthrightness of any absolutes.

Here, for example, is Burns asserting his own sense of what values are: "Values indicate desirable or preferred *end-states* or collective goals or explicit purposes, and values are *standards* in terms of which specific criteria may be established and choices made among alternatives" (74). Burns is clearly trying to keep his definition wide enough open to include most of what the ordinary American would think of as a value or values. But in doing so, he avoids the critical question of agency—who, exactly, does the desiring and the preferring in his phrase "desirable or preferred *end-states*"? He answers this question indirectly as he enumerates other aspects—or alternatives?—of what a value is by adding, "or collective goals or explicit purposes. . . ." The question of whether a value is different—perhaps better—if held by many rather than by one, seems to suggest itself here, but Burns won't engage it, except indirectly as he talks about standards. Even here, though, the question of just whose standards he's talking about obscures, at least for me, the bit of ground his definitions seek to clear.

Burns would not take his lack of moral positivism as a limit to the value of his ideas; he would point, as he points at most junctures in *Leadership*, to people more directly involved in the teaching of ethics for the real goods in that regard, and note that he is not trying to do what they have done well enough themselves. Directly following a discussion of Kohlberg's theories of the stages of moral development, Burns writes that "It is in the congruence of levels of need and other motivations, and of the stages of moral development, that leadership is animated, politicized, and enlivened with moral purpose" (73). Putting aside the overwhelming vagueness of the opening clause about "levels of need and other motivations," it seems that Burns is saying that from the definitions of the good that

Kohlberg finds the most advanced people to share, good leadership takes its moral substance. What does Kohlberg find people believing at the highest stage of moral development? Here is Kohlberg answering that question: "Self-chosen principles. . . . Principles are universal principles of justice: the equality of human rights and respect for the dignity of human beings as individual persons" (9). Kohlberg means by self-chosen not that the individual makes up the core principles herself, but that she freely chooses to adhere to the "universal" principals. But these universal principles say little—what exactly is it, in practical terms that one would offer a student of leadership, that respects the dignity of human beings as individual persons?

There is a kernel of real substance here, though, and that is the notion of equality of human rights. Nevertheless, Kohlberg never talks about how one is to distinguish between a right and, for example, a privilege, or a right and an opportunity, or a right and a freedom.

Trapped within this fundamental relativism of Kohlberg's model of moral development, Burns's definition of transforming leadership cannot explain King.

As I see it, King instead explains Burns. Why do we recognize the power of Burns's definition of transforming leadership? Because Burns comes as close as any academic relying on the indirect moral vision of social science *can* come to the overwhelming sights of faith. What Burns does not say outright, but what many readers will take from his discussion of leadership nonetheless, is that the best leaders operate on the souls of their followers. They do this by putting forth ideas about the nature of the essential good, and by making the good more palpable for their followers.

It is clearly not the role of the college to try to improve the souls of its students in this way. But the college can and should talk about the way leaders seek to operate on their souls; the college can, should, and must let its students know that their ideas and their beliefs will be courted by all who seek to lead them. We need to help our students understand that the best leadership speaks honestly to their intellects, as King always did. If our students are to lead, let us teach them to speak the language of ideas as King spoke the language of ideas. If they are to follow, let us teach them to listen for the respect of mind and soul that King offered as well.

Notes

1. Bass uses the term "transformational leader," borrowed from Burns, and which I will discuss in greater detail at the end of this article. Burns was more willing than Bass generally is to engage in a discussion of the moral dimensions of leadership, but even Burns allows his admiration for leadership technique to overwhelm his moral sensibility. The glaring example in his book *Leadership* is his admiration for Mao's accomplishments in affecting so many so profoundly through the cultural revolution. Certainly it is more than the advantage of hindsight that allows the critical reader to wonder why Burns ignores the moral significance of that revolution.

2. In fairness, I should point out that Bass does make passing reference to Abraham Maslow as a moral touchstone, but the same criticism applies to Maslow as well—if one is "self-actualized," one is not necessarily good.

Works Cited

Bass, Bernard M. *Bass and Stogdill's Handbook of Leadership: Theory, Research, and Managerial Application*. 3e. New York: Free Press, 1990.

Burns, James MacGregor. *Leadership*. New York: Harper & Row, 1978.

King, Martin Luther, Jr. *Why We Can't Wait*. New York: Harper, 1964.

Kohlberg, Lawrence, F. Clark Power, and Ann Higgens. *Lawrence Kohlberg's Approach to Moral Education*. New York: Columbia University Press, 1989.

Maslow, Abraham. *Motivation and Personality*. New York: Harper, 1954.

Rauschenbusch, Walter. *Christianity and the Social Crisis*. New York: Macmillan,

5

Plato's *Republic* as Leadership Text

Paul F. Johnson

Students are invariably surprised—and pleasantly so—upon first opening Plato's *Republic* and beginning to read. At some point along the way in their schooling they have heard the august names of Socrates and Plato piously invoked in connection with some obscure and daunting philosophical claim, and so come to associate them with a mysterious and esoteric realm of profound ruminations. Socrates and Plato themselves are fleshed out in the imagination as the gray-haired bearded giants of ancient Greek philosophy: god-like, unapproachable, severe. They are surprised to discover that Socrates himself never wrote anything, never held any position at a college or university, or responsible position in society at all, and never even pretended to have any deep philosophical insights to offer. He spent his days shambling about the streets of Athens, devoted only to the gentle art of conversational inquiry with others of his time who were curious to know the truth. They are surprised at the welcoming and congenial tone of Plato's dialogue format, the humor and wit of the people they find engaged in the dialogue, and the vividness of the personalities who emerge in the course of conversation. And they are most especially surprised to find that the issues explored in *Republic* are not at all mysterious and esoteric but very similar to questions that they have themselves encountered, and worried about, and tried to think through. The opening pages of *Republic* offer an almost irresistible invitation to join into discussion with some very likable folk on topics of interest to almost anyone with a modicum of curiosity about the perplexities of human affairs. It's all quite disarming.

As a text for leadership studies courses, *Republic* offers many advantages. Not least among these is the ease with which leadership topics can be brought into the classroom for serious and lively engagement. The topics addressed are very wide ranging indeed and, despite its ancient vintage, *Republic* speaks to issues that are also of intense personal concern to today's young people. It offers psychological insights into the deeper workings of human motivation, advances some startling claims about love and marriage and child rearing that have a stark relevance for contemporary society, and challenges reflection on the nature of the relationship between the individual and the state. Through it all Plato maintains his focus on certain core moral questions that go to the very heart of the leadership question. What is the good life for a human being? What does a just society look like? Who should lead and why? Plato will attempt to provide answers to these questions, and students have little difficulty in speaking their minds in response to the various arguments that are developed along the way. *Republic* is, of course, a dialogue, and the conversational format of the text invites all readers to participate by voicing their own opinions, whether to agree or disagree, and in either case the reactions tend to be quite lively. In a very real sense, the students themselves become participants in the conversation between Socrates and his young friends, engaged in a common effort to inquire after answers to some of life's most enduring questions. The effect can be truly remarkable.

One should perhaps be careful, however, not to underestimate the challenge which this text presents. Some of the arguments are terribly complex, there are long stretches of crabbed distinction-mongering, and various tangents that seem only remotely connected to the main topic. To use *Republic* effectively as a leadership text requires some willingness to cast a wide net, and to consider discussions which may or may not bear some significance for the general direction of the classroom discussion. There is no good way to predict the topics or the general course of argument that a given class will find compelling—and no two classes are likely to be the same. As an example of this sort of thing one might consider the long digression, which occurs from the middle of Book Two to the middle of Book Three, on the importance of popular culture, especially popular music, within society. Plato recognized the enormous potential which the "poets" had to influence the young through the power of musical rhythm and lyrics. Now, for one class this topic would require serious attention, and could very readily be adapted to the themes of leadership; for another it would be hardly relevant at all. And *Republic* is well stocked with topic areas such as this. More generally, *Republic* requires, on the part of the instructor, a certain confidence in her students and even some courage in herself, precisely because one can hardly know beforehand where the class will go with the text, or what results to expect. I personally count this as a further advantage because it keeps everyone, including the instructor, on their toes. But for those who have a particular view of leadership to advocate, or for those who are looking for a cut-and-dried theory of leadership *Republic* is probably not a wise choice.

Having said as much, I don't mean to leave the impression that *Republic* offers nothing more than a sort of leadership Rorschach test—one can see in it almost anything one pleases—or that adopting it for a leadership studies course amounts to a philosophical crap-shoot. Plato has some rather clear notions about who should accede to positions of authority and why, notions which are deeply controversial. But one needn't agree with Plato, of course, to find value in his arguments. Reading *Republic* challenges students to place their own opinions and ideas in question, to find reasons and arguments for the things they believe, and to come to recognize that there are important alternatives that need to be considered. The real value of the book for leadership studies consists in the fact that it brings the most contentious issues of leadership directly to the fore and puts students into contact with the deeper moral questions that must attend any theoretical approach to leadership in the contemporary world. In the pages to follow I should like to adduce several of the most prominent themes to be encountered in *Republic*, making no claim to the completeness of my list or the necessity of pursuing just these. As I've said, different classes will tend in different directions, though the themes I've chosen to discuss should provide a few landmarks for what is, after all, a very richly textured piece of conceptual terrain.

1. Leadership begins at home: The state-soul analogy

The main argument of *Republic* is built around an analogy between the political order at large and the individual human soul. Socrates and his friends have raised the question, "What is justice?" and it is generally agreed that justice can be found in two different places. There are just persons and there are just states. It would make sense as an argumentative strategy to investigate the larger of these two because it is likely that the elements which work together to produce justice could be more easily discerned there. "Perhaps," says Socrates, "there is more justice in the larger thing, and it will be easier to learn what it is. So, if you're willing, let's first find out what sort of thing justice is in a city and afterwards look for it in the individual, observing the ways in which the smaller is similar to the larger" (369a).[1] As it turns out, the argument does not proceed quite so directly as we are given here to expect, but the mapping of structure from the one entity, the state, onto the other, the soul, is relatively straightforward.

Human beings, on the view advanced by Socrates, are essentially social creatures. We are more akin to beavers, bees, and ants than we are to leopards, polar bears or red-tailed hawks. The reason for this is that no one person is entirely self-sufficient, no one can adequately provide for herself the various things that she needs for survival and comfort. Each of us has, however, some one specific talent, or some peculiar configuration of talents which enables us to do a specific task exceedingly well. Cultivating the soil and raising a crop requires one set of abilities, carpentry another; one person is good with words, the next with numbers, and so on. By pooling our talents and coming together to form a community, we can establish a system of reciprocal dependency wherein each person can make a contribution to the welfare of others and expect them to do the same in return. By dividing our labors, each person can devote himself to the perfection of whatever skill he finds himself capable of mastering and hence become so much the more productive. Our natural lack of self-sufficiency thus becomes the basis for communal life and for the maximization of productive capacity of the community itself. So far so good.

But the very efficiency of this system of reciprocal labor generates a new problem. The minute our new community begins to generate a surplus and can begin to devote itself to the production of luxury goods it must concern itself with the possibility that other communities in the area will grow envious of our wealth and commence expropriatory action against us. We will need to find "a few good men" (actually, "persons," because Plato explicitly includes women in his treatment here) who, by virtue of their athletic capabilities and high-spiritedness, will be able to defend us against attack. Some small segment of the population shall have to be separated from the basic tasks of production and form themselves into an army. These persons will be the strongest, most cunning and aggressive of our community, and they will be trained and provided with the weapons required to do their job. They emerge as a wholly distinct class within our community with a specific task assigned to them. But this raises still another problem: how can we be sure that they won't turn against the home population and subject them to their will? What's to prevent them from going on the offensive and attacking other communities? Their very presence within the polity, while solving one problem, raises yet another, and potentially more serious one.

In response to this new liability, Socrates argues for the need of a third class of individuals whose function it shall be to provide governance over the soldiery, and we come, by these steps, to our first encounter with the issues involved with leadership. Socrates maintains that, just as the soldiers are drawn from the wider population, so too these new leaders must be drawn from the ranks of the soldiers themselves, as a subset of this subset of the community at large. We shall identify those who have the necessary characteristics for leadership by subjecting the soldiers to a battery of tests: We shall expose them to violent dangers, entice them with all manner of temptation, give them every opportunity to relinquish their duties and tasks in favor of their own perceived better interests. The steadfastness required to resist such temptations, to maintain oneself unfailingly in one's appointed station and to affirm in all situations the higher interests of one's community in preference to one's own is a rare quality indeed, and only a very few will be found to possess it. And these, we can be assured, are the ones with "the right stuff" for leadership.

The human community, then, will form itself by a sort of natural progression into a three-tiered, hierarchical order. There is the vast majority of society devoted to the special tasks required for the production of basic needs: Socrates calls these the "artisans"; there are the soldiers who will see to the common defense: the "auxiliaries"; and there are the select few at the top who see to the maintenance of the whole arrangement: the "guardians." At this point, very little has actually been said about the specific qualities which make for a good leader, but this concern is only deferred to a slightly later point in the argument that we will come to in just a moment. The whole discussion among Socrates and the others has been devoted to identifying justice, and the state, as the larger of the two entities in which justice might be found, was thought to provide a better specimen for examination than the individual soul. Now, according to the traditional value-system at work in Athens at the time, there were four cardinal virtues, moderation, courage, wisdom, and justice. Socrates and his friends now find themselves in a position to make some provisional claims about what justice is by locating it within their "city in speech." They begin by locating the other three virtues: wisdom will of course pertain to the small class of guardians, though it remains to be seen wherein consists their special wisdom; courage, obviously enough, will be the special virtue of the soldier class; and moderation, though it is a virtue that all members of the community will need to possess if we are to have any good prospects of survival, is the virtue which the artisans shall have especially to cultivate. And justice? It is that virtue which pervades the whole social structure and represents the willingness of all persons within society, regardless of their station, to do their own job. Justice, it turns out, is a sort of harmony of the parts, a harmony attained by the recognition on the part of all persons that the three-tiered structure of their community is in accordance with nature, that everyone has a specific task to do and must respect and trust all others to do their own work. Knowing one's place in society, and committing oneself to perform one's task to the utmost of one's ability without meddling in the business of others will produce a social order which is efficient, viable and, most important, just.

In order to pursue the further question of what makes for a genuine leader, Socrates proposes to inquire whether the results achieved so far regarding the nature of justice within the state can be transposed to the case of the individual human being, and this is where the strategy of analogy comes into play. If we look within ourselves, Socrates suggests, we will find three distinct elements which correspond, roughly, to the three social classes. The "appetitive" element comprises all the organic and biological functions within us which are devoted to basic survival and the maintenance of good health: the appetites for food and drink, for commodious shelter against the elements, and for the reproduction of our kind. This element corresponds to the class within society devoted to the procurement and production of our basic necessities, and is by far the largest and the most obstreperous and unruly part of the soul. But it does not always simply get its way. We very often have an appetite for something that we know we mustn't have. The appetites themselves make no such distinction between the things we desire and the things it would be well for us to have, and so Socrates posits the existence within us of a calculating, or "rational" part of our souls whose function it is to make the decision between those appetites which may properly be indulged and those which must be denied, or indulged to only a certain extent. This element corresponds to the guardian class. But there is also a third element within the soul, what Socrates calls the "spirited" part, which is neither entirely rational nor merely appetitive. It is perhaps the most difficult one to describe, and Socrates only tells us that it is "the spirited part by which we get angry." (439e) This is not altogether satisfactory, of course, but I think everyone knows what it is to feel in "high spirits," to be energized and vigorous, or "in the zone" of high performance. We need only recognize that such states are neither "rational" nor "appetitive" in order to grant the point, provisionally, that there is some third element within each of us which, while distinct, is nonetheless closely related to the other two. Besides anger we might include such other affective states as joy, depression (in the case of "low" spirits), confidence, and even boredom to help us identify that part of ourselves which complements ratiocination and appetite.

The soul, then, evinces the same three-part structure as the state. Each person has all three elements within them, though people tend to possess them in different proportions. Examples of the different types are not hard to adduce. We all know people for whom good food and drink, fine homes and fast cars, and exquisite sex constitute the primary objectives in life: these are the ones whose appetitive element is more or less running the show. Other persons are highly competitive and derive their greatest satisfaction in throwing themselves into the fray, developing their strengths and energies to as high a level as possible, testing their limits, seeking thrills and adventure above all else, and subordinating all else to such pursuits. These are the ones whose spirited element is predominant. Still others are given to contemplation, to the life of the mind, people who find their greatest delight in ideas and culture and books. Their rational element is by far the most highly developed, and the other two are relegated to a position of subordination. Just as in the state each social class has an important function to serve, so too each of the elements within the soul has its appropriate function, and just as in the state justice is found to consist in a certain harmony and balance between the classes which permits of their cooperation and mutual respect, justice within the soul also consists in our bringing these three elements into harmony with each other, allowing each to have its special role while constraining any part which might seek to overreach its appointed function. And here again, it's not hard to spot people who have failed to attain a proper sense of balance among their soul's elements. If the appetites hold sway for too long a person is apt to grow avaricious and overindulgent, leading, in the extreme cases, to social isolation and the slow deterioration of the body. Competitive types grow harsh and brutal and cruel. Rational types become captious and sanctimonious and soft. To avoid such distortions of character, all three elements must be given due respect and allowed to participate in its formation. Only in this way will a person come to be moderate, courageous, and wise and, ultimately, just.

But how is one to do that? How does one reign in one's appetites, or suppress the instinctive urge to compete, or moderate one's indulgence in intellectual pursuits? It is in answer to this question that Socrates takes the further step in addressing what we have so far adduced as the issue of leadership. There is one passage in particular in *Republic* where the interworkings of the three elements of the soul are presented with great force and clarity:

> Socrates: What happens when a person thinks that he has done something unjust? Isn't it true that the nobler he is, the less he resents it if he suffers hunger or cold, or the like at the hands of someone whom he believes to be inflicting this on him justly, and won't his spirit, as I say, refuse to be aroused?
> Glaucon: That's true.
> Socrates: But what happens if, instead, he believes that someone has been unjust to him? Isn't the spirit within him boiling and angry, fighting for what he believes to be just? Won't it endure hunger, cold, and the like and keep on till it is victorious, not ceasing from noble actions until it either wins, dies, or calms down, called to heel by the reason within him, like a dog by a shepherd?
> Glaucon: Spirit is certainly like that. (440c–d)

The key notion in this passage is the knowledge or belief that one has either committed or suffered an injustice in relation to other persons. As we have seen, the appetitive element within the soul is by far the largest, and spirit too is capable of overwhelming dominance. Reason is in general the smallest part of our soul, and the question we asked a moment ago, How is it possible to achieve the sort of harmony of elements that justice requires, can be restated thus: How is it ever possible that the appetites and spirit should ever be controlled? (Even in cases of the contemplative type of person whose reason has got the upper hand, some aspect of one's reason must recognize the need to cultivate the other elements.) Socrates offers us two cases in the passage above: if I know that I have done something wrong or unjust, then my spirit remains docile when someone comes to punish me—that is, when my free pursuit of my appetites is infringed ("hunger or cold, or the like . . ."). Or again, if I believe that someone has done me wrong, spirit becomes aroused and wholly supersedes the demands of appetite in trying to put things right. In both cases, reason, in possession of some type of knowledge (knowledge of what is just) is able to call spirit into alliance with itself and together they are able to control appetite. Reason must impose some form of discipline within the soul in order to achieve the necessary balance and harmony of the parts, but this discipline is only possible, reason is only able to effect control over the lower elements by virtue of its possession of this peculiar form of knowledge regarding right and wrong. Moreover, it is precisely those people who are able to attain such knowledge, and thereby attain justice within their own souls who are worthy to assume the position of guardian within the community. Both forms of justice, then, justice within the soul and justice within the state, are contingent upon the attainment of a certain form of knowledge. The true leader within the human community is the one who has come into possession of this knowledge and demonstrated her possession of it through the justice she manifests in all her actions, in all her dealings with other people. To prove oneself worthy of leadership, then, is to have achieved mastery over oneself. One can only presume to lead others when one has proven the ability to "lead" oneself. Leadership begins at home, as it were.

But what sort of knowledge is it that is required, first, for self-mastery, and second, for legitimate leadership according to Socrates?

2. Leadership and moral knowledge: two similes

It is apparent from the passage above that Socrates is talking about our knowledge of the distinction between right and wrong. (Plato uses the terms "just" and "unjust," but his meaning is clear, and his use of these terms needn't give rise to the seeming problem of circularity they may imply.) When we ask ourselves, or when students are asked where we get our sense of right and wrong the most natural response (and the one students are likely to offer) is that our "society" gives them to us through the process of education and acculturation. Children are instructed by their parents, who were similarly instructed by their own and have the added advantage of having lived their lives in the real world where ethical values have currency. If my society tells me that something is impermissible or wrong, I had better conform my behavior to the patterns of conduct which its standards impose. If other cultures think otherwise, if, for example, other cultures permit a man to have several wives, that is well within their rights, and there is no point in trying to decide whose culture gets it right. There simply is no higher standard to which one might appeal in trying to make that judgment. Cultural relativism has so thoroughly gained sway over our thinking in these matters as to have all but eliminated from our consideration any other ways of marking ethical distinctions. But a moment's reflection soon shows the liabilities to which cultural relativism is subject. There seem to be cases of certain cultural practices that are just simply wrong (the case of Nazi Germany comes only too readily to mind), but if cultural relativism is correct, then our sense of their wrongness is just one big mistake. Or again, even internal to our own culture, there are practices and hard choices for which the prevailing cultural ethos seems less than authoritative or settled. Abortion, affirmative action, or any number of hard cases in the realm of biomedical practice challenge us to say where the line between right and wrong lies, and it is only a sort of bias, or lazy unreflectiveness that would permit one to think that our society itself provides the standard of ethical valuations. But if cultural relativism is so easily thrown into question, how else is there to approach the problems of morality?

There is no better way to confront our students today with this issue than by a careful reading of *Republic*, because Plato thoroughly rejects relativism of any stripe and goes a very long way indeed in his attempt to provide a viable alternative. Plato's alternative, very briefly, is that the world itself is pervaded by an ordering principle—the *logos*—which brings order out of chaos, establishes the regularity and beauty that we perceive in nature, and regulates all facets of reality with a consistency and immutability that underlies all apparent change and flux. Mathematics is a manifestation of the *logos*, but, according to Plato, the same veracity and timelessness which pertain to the principles of geometry and mathematics can be found to support our intuitive awareness of the existence of moral order in the world. In the later stages of *Republic*, Plato introduces his Theory of Forms, and argues that the Form of the Good is the principle which brings order and harmony and certainty into our moral lives in the same way that mathematics can disclose the order and regularity of the universe itself.[2] The principles of moral conduct are no more the product of the society in which we happen to be living than is the Pythagorean Theorem. Our moral inquiries should be thought of as a process of discovering a reality which is there to be revealed, just as the mathematician is involved by her researches in the process of discovering—*discovering*, not inventing—the immutable structure of mathematical relationships. It is through the use of our reason alone that the truth is discovered in the latter domain; it is by reason, too, that we come to know of the reality of the moral principles which ought to govern our lives.

The Theory of Forms is of course a very subtle and sophisticated construction, and the foregoing summary is only intended to give the general sense of the thing. It is assuredly not beyond the competence of any devoted student to understand, and its plausibility derives precisely from its ability to respond to the seeming inadequacy of relativistic moral theory. In order to resume our own discussion of the leadership issue as it emerges from the pages of *Republic*, I propose to examine two similes—arresting in their simplicity and power—which Plato offers as a way of illustrating the moral perspective he advocates. These similes have to do with the nature of leadership as it may be practiced within the state—political leadership—but it will enable us to return, in the next section, to what should probably appear to be a prior question, "leadership" within the soul. As we will see, the two forms of leadership are actually internally connected in such a way as to disallow any such prioritizing of one form over the other.

The first is the Simile of the Beast. Socrates here is arguing against people who think and teach that ethics is only a matter of public opinion, and who advocate the learning of the skills of persuasive speech as a way of getting the best out of life. But listen carefully and his words can be found to apply only too easily to much of what passes for political leadership today:

> Not one of those paid private teachers, whom the people call sophists . . . teaches anything other than the convictions that the majority express when they are gathered together. Indeed, these are precisely

what the sophists call wisdom. It's as if someone were learning the moods and appetites of a huge, strong beast that he's rearing—how to approach and handle it, when it is most difficult to deal with or most gentle and what makes it so, what sounds it utters in either condition, and what sounds soothe or anger it. Having learned all this through tending the beast over a period of time, he calls this knack wisdom, gathers his information together as if it were a craft, and starts to teach it. In truth, he knows nothing about which of these convictions is fine or shameful, good or bad, just or unjust, but he applies all these names in accordance with how the beast reacts—calling what it enjoys good and what angers it bad. He has no other account to give of these terms. (493a–c)

Plato might just as well have been describing the way our politicians today consult the public opinion polls before making the slightest pronouncement about their own policy recommendations or positions. Wet a finger and poke it into the prevailing cultural winds and you will know what the people want, and what they think is right. That may be sage advice for politicians today, but it in no way relieves us of the obligation to ask whether the majority's sense of right and wrong is *really* correct. There was a time in our own country when it was the people's will to keep minority students segregated from the white majority, and "the beast" had no inclination whatsoever to change its views. That doesn't make segregation right, and Socrates is only trying to bring that hard fact into the light of day. But if majority sentiment does not make it right, why not? and what does? Consider next the second simile, the Ship of State:

> Imagine that something like the following happens on a ship or on many ships.... The sailors are quarreling with one another about steering the ship, each of them thinking that he should be the captain, even though he's never learned the art of navigation, cannot point to anyone who taught it to him, or to a time when he learned it. Indeed, they claim that it isn't teachable and are ready to cut to pieces anyone who says that it is. They're always crowding around the ship owner, begging him and doing everything possible to get him to turn the rudder over to them. And sometimes, if they don't succeed in persuading him, they execute the ones who do succeed or throw them overboard, and then, having stupefied their noble ship owner with drugs, wine, or in some other way, they rule the ship, using up what's in it and sailing in the way that people like that are prone to do. Moreover, they call the person who is clever at persuading or forcing the

ship owner to let them rule a "navigator," a "captain," and "one who knows ships," and dismiss anyone else as useless. They don't understand that a true captain must pay attention to the seasons of the year, the sky, the stars, the winds, and all that pertains to his craft, if he's really to be the ruler of a ship. And they don't believe there is any craft that would enable him to determine where he should steer the ship to, independently of whether the others want to go there or not, or any possibility of mastering this alleged craft or of practicing it at the same time as the craft of navigation. Don't you think that the true captain will be called a real stargazer, a babbler, and a good-for-nothing by those who sail in ships governed in that way, in which such things happen? (488a–e)

These two similes are directed towards the establishment of a common point: that there is an important distinction to be made between persuasion which is based solely on the power of eloquent speech or manipulation and persuasion which follows from the mutual recognition of the truth. We are in a position to draw a first conclusion regarding the nature of leadership as Plato would have the thing understood: that *leadership cannot be thought to consist solely in effective techniques* for bringing people to agree with any given proposal of a course of action. In the case of the sailors and the hapless ship owner, Socrates is claiming that the desire to lead is often nothing more than the desire to put oneself into possession of the means to secure the various things that the appetites are clamoring for. The primary objective here is only to have a surfeit of pleasurable goods to the complete neglect of where the collective best interests of society may lie. Everyone on board the ship may succeed in having a howling good time, but the ship itself drifts hither and yon at the mercy of aimless winds and currents. Now, in a democratic society the "ship owner" is ostensibly the people themselves, and, with a little imagination, Plato's image can be interpreted to apply to the current state of Western democracies in general. The ship owner—the people— is seduced into acquiescence by the sailors' doling out all manner of goodies to make him—us—feel satisfied with the day-to-day administration of the vessel. Our current budget deficits correspond to the sailors' "using up what's in the ship" while paying little attention to whither our ship is tending. We are all made to feel basically content and well taken care of as we drift ever closer to the shoals that will shatter the mainbeams of our little boat.

Meanwhile, at the rear deck of the ship there stand a few "useless babblers" and "stargazers" who direct their attention to the skies and climatic conditions that have a genuine significance for the general bearing of the ship. The simile here is intending to draw a comparison between the discernible facts of astronomy and meteorology which are crucial to navigation and the principles of morality which ought to hold sway in the governance of the political order. The point here is that the stars are useful and necessary for navigation precisely because they do not move, they offer a stationary frame of reference within the context of which the position of the ship relative to geographical coordinates can be determined. According to Plato's Theory of Forms, the realm of the forms themselves provide a similar frame of reference for our moral and political judgments. Like the stars, the principles of moral conduct are stationary and unchanging; they provide the necessary frame of reference which allows us to take our moral bearings as we seek to navigate the ship of state in the directions we choose to go. And, like the stargazers on the ship, the people within society who have acquired the knowledge of the forms will be the ones who are needed to provide guidance even though they seem devoted to the study of things that most people do not understand and are criticized as useless prattlers and nags. It is by virtue of their special knowledge and skills that they are needed, but because the knowledge they have accrues to them only as the result of careful study and devotion to task, the people who need their guidance have no clear sense of what it is they have to offer.

Owing to this ignorance, the people are especially vulnerable to the claims of those who reject the existence of moral principle in favor of popular opinion and cultural trends. The Simile of the Beast offers us a literary image of the demagogues and "spinmeisters" of our own day as the "trainer" who seeks only to control and manipulate the populace in its lugubrious disquiet. One is reluctant, beyond a certain point, to allow Plato's literary devices to carry too much of the argument, but the point we can safely draw here is that, in the absence of any appeal to moral principle public discourse is reduced to special interest pleading and rhetorical manipulation. Plato forces us to recognize the liabilities we face if we eschew the hard work of trying to articulate the basic principles which inform and support our communal existence. There are liabilities to confront in the other direction as well: Advocacy of principle can too readily go over into dogmatism and intolerance, and, with respect to Plato's own recommendations, we should be sensitive to the fact that the Theory of Forms is itself subject to all manner of philosophical dispute. But again, the point is not to agree with Plato. Reading *Republic* is only a very effective means of bringing to the attention of our students the primary alternatives available to us as we strive to understand the problems we face and the conditions of public engagement with the issues. On the point of leadership, Plato reminds us that mere technique and the mastery of political stratagems are in no way sufficient unto themselves as means to determine the direction we might choose to pursue in our political lives together. Leadership, on his view, must always be informed and buttressed by moral understanding and wisdom. But there is something more which needs to be said about the nature of the moral knowledge which he argues is essential to genuine leadership.

3. The method of leadership: listening and speaking

There is one crucial aspect of Plato's conception of leadership which we must be careful not to ignore. The persons capable of genuine leadership within any given society will always be a very small minority, an elite. And Plato, famously, is no great friend of democracy. Nevertheless, I believe that both Plato's conception of leadership (the "philosopher-king") and the special form of knowledge which he claims such a person must have to be qualified for leadership can be interpreted in ways which makes them more conducive to contemporary circumstances. The interpretations I offer here make leadership a practice available to a larger range of persons than Plato might endorse, and his conception of knowledge—knowledge of the Forms—can be seen to arise from a specific method which is actually quite consistent with a democratic form of governance.

The argument of *Republic* proceeds on two separate levels. So far our discussion has been devoted almost exclusively to what might be called the "discursive" level of presentation, having to do primarily with the actual substance of the arguments developed by Socrates and his friends. The second level of argument—what I'll call the "dramatic" level—complements the discursive features by offering us an illustration of the method that Socrates used, and which Plato himself appropriates. Through the power of his literary art, Plato is able to make various important claims in support of the major argument through the setting, the personalities and the dramatic events which constitute the dialogic form of *Republic*. For example, in the opening pages Socrates begins a conversation on the topic of justice with Cephalus, an elderly citizen of Athens who is preparing to do homage to the gods. Cephalus is a successful man and fits the image of what Athenian society would expect of a just and pious soul. But when Socrates begins to probe him about the actual conception of justice that he has attempted to abide in living a decent life, Cephalus is reluctant to say on, and simply declines to engage with Socrates in the investigation that might ensue. He gives the argument over to his son, Polemarchus, who is anxious to explore with Socrates the real meaning of justice. By this simple dramatic device, Plato shows us that questions regarding the nature of morality are ones that must be addressed anew by each succeeding generation as they are still only preparing themselves to take their places within society. There is no need actually to come out and say that each generation of young persons must open themselves to such inquiry, the point being made in terms of dramatic structure and action. Such elements are present at every turn in the discursive argument, and the reader should be alert to the ancillary points that Plato is making at this dramatic level.

The primary substance of the main argument of the text is Plato's attempt to refute and provide an alternative to the creeping moral relativism which he viewed as the gravest of threats to the continued health of the Athenian polity. His alternative might be called moral objectivism, consisting in the attempt to establish a standard of moral adjudication which is universal, immutable, and demonstrable. These two contrasting views of morality, relativism, and objectivism, are each affiliated with their own style of public discourse. If, according to the relativist, there are no moral absolutes, then the thing to do is learn how to make the most plausible and compelling case for whatever position one might care to advance. Accordingly, one should master the techniques of public speech-making, rhetoric, the better to persuade a listening audience to align their interests with one's own. This is not, of course, the style of discourse that Socrates employs. The "Socratic method" consists in a process of questioning and answering, and makes certain demands of anyone who would willingly engage in a conversation directed at finding out the truth. And it is here, in connection with the protocols of Socratic method, that I believe the more important point regarding Plato's conception of knowledge is to be found. Even though Socrates will ultimately be made to espouse the Theory of Forms, he himself never claims to have attained complete knowledge of the Forms, but only insists that he has devoted his life to its pursuit. *He cannot do this by himself.* He requires the active and willing participation of other persons who are prepared to advance their own opinions in response to the questions it occurs to him to ask as the process of investigation goes forward. If there are to be any good hopes for the process of inquiry to make progress in the direction of knowledge, all participants in the discussion must evince certain attitudes and characteristics. They must, first of all, be prepared to acknowledge that their own opinions may be mistaken and willing to subject their deepest convictions to probing inspection. This is not usually an easy or comfortable thing to do. They must be willing at all times to say what they think, honestly and candidly, about matters of deepest personal concern. And they must have the alacrity and clear-headedness to follow the twists and turns the argument is likely to take, and the perceptiveness to mark whatever distinctions may be introduced along the way. If all of these conditions are met, Socrates has found his element, and all parties to the discussion can reasonably expect movement in the direction of better knowledge. And what is it that will mark the approach toward, or the arrival at truth? Rational consent, mutual agreement among the parties after an exhaustive and painstaking search into alternatives. Persuasion, in the only legitimate sense of the word.

On these terms we can reconsider more carefully the question we have so long deferred. What is it that makes for a good leader? Precisely the skills that make for serious, analytical, and congenial engagement in public discourse. The philosopher-king is no isolated pedant sitting off in his ivory tower somewhere, nor an unapproachable paragon of wisdom who pontificates and condescends to the uninformed rabble who stand with upturned faces to receive his profundity. Rather, the person fit to lead is the person who knows how to listen to a good argument, who is willing to offer her own views when queried, and who acknowledges the imperative to engage with others in the common pursuit of the truth. To understand Plato's conception of the "guardian," the genuine leader, the "philosopher-king," we need to appreciate the Greek meaning of the very term "philosopher." The word means a "lover of wisdom," and to love something does not require that one be in full possession of that which one loves. Indeed, it may be a necessary requirement of genuine love that one *does not possess* the thing one loves. The Theory of Forms can be interpreted to mean only that there is a truth out there to be pursued, and that by diligent effort we may hope at least to move toward proximity to it. Subjecting ourselves to the discipline of the methods that Socrates himself practices will in any event help us to resist the constant temptation of dogmatism and forestall the ascendancy of the tyranny of righteousness. Leadership is a cooperative effort that takes us further along the path from ignorance to wisdom, engaged in mutual respect for others involved in its pursuit and for the objective that we must seek to attain though it may forever lie just beyond our grasp. To know the truth is to search for it, and we cannot search alone.

These, I think, are the salient lessons to be drawn from a careful reading of Plato's *Republic*. The topics covered here are treated only in outline, and there are so many more that can be discovered in the company of bright young minds who will never cease to find something new in this inexhaustible text. There is, perhaps, an argument to be made here for the necessity of embedding the study of leadership within the context of a liberal arts education. I'll leave that for another occasion. The emergence of leadership studies as a new and vigorous field of study is evidence of the perceived need for a more thorough and incisive investigation of the dynamics of human interaction. One can hardly do better, in one's initial approach to the issues which leadership studies define, than to refresh oneself with an immersion in the humane and humanizing waters of ancient philosophy.

Notes

1. I am using the Grube translation (Hackett Publishing, 1992) of *Republic*, and shall make all citations in the body of my essay. References are to the Stephanus pagination, which are usually provided with any translation of Plato.

2. For a more detailed treatment of Plato's Theory of Forms, please see my other essay in the present volume.

6

Understanding Destructive Obedience: The Milgram Experiments

Mark E. Sibicky

Obedience to authority presents an interesting dilemma to anyone interested in studying leadership. On the one hand, obedience to authority is necessary for the proper functioning of any complex hierarchical society, such as the type found in the United States. On the other hand, while necessary, obedience to authority also has a dark and destructive side.

The systematic extermination of Jews by the Nazis, the massacre of innocent civilians at My Lai in Vietnam, the ordered mass suicides of religious cult members, and recent nerve gas attacks on Japanese subway passengers by cult members are just some examples of destructive obedience in the twentieth century. In my experience, students have little difficulty adding to this list of examples. What is difficult for them is to come to an understanding of why someone could obey such destructive orders.

As social scientists know, the reasons underlying destructive obedience are often complex, and yet, my very intelligent students routinely give me similar and very simple explanations as to why someone would obey destructive orders. In general, my students focus on the dispositional character of subordinates, while disregarding any role that social-situational factors may play in influencing obedience. The most common explanations I receive from students, and I might add from many colleagues, can be summarized by the following statement: "A good, or normal person would know better and disobey a harmful order. Those who do obey harmful orders must be bad or stupid."

This tendency to focus on the internal dispositions of obedient subordinates while underestimating situational influences is known to social psychologists as the fundamental attribution error (see Ross). Although the fundamental attribution error is prevalent among people in Western societies, it still, in my opinion, detracts from my students' understanding of the social phenomenon of obedience. I should mention that I am not denying that personality may play some role in obedience, rather I am suggesting that most people overemphasize personality as an explanation and fail to consider social-situational factors. My own inadequacies as a teacher aside, getting students to consider the complexity of obedience and take part in a critical and mindful analysis of obedience is not an easy task. One way I have attempted to engage students in this process is to introduce them to Stanley Milgram's work on obedience.

In a series of classic experiments, Milgram demonstrated that "good" and ordinary people can be induced, against their nature, to cause harm to an innocent victim; all because they were ordered to do so by an authority figure. Milgram's research is important because it demonstrates the power and influence that social situations can have over people. Although Milgram's research may be familiar to some students in leadership studies courses, I find that most students are unaware of some important aspects of his findings and their implications. For example, many students believe that Milgram simply showed how easily people will obey an authority figure. In truth, his work goes well beyond this point, providing insights into the way we perceive people who obey and demonstrating several social-situational factors that can affect the probability of destructive obedience occurring.

What follows is a description of the issues and techniques I use to introduce students to Milgram's work and my attempts to engage them in more mindful discussion of his work. I also present a synopsis of Milgram's research paradigm and an overview of his relevant findings and conclusions.

Researchers in the United States have found that the dominant image—or "implicit theory"—of what constitutes an ideal leader tends to be slanted toward a masculine image and also includes such traits as aggressiveness, self-confidence, competitiveness, and independence (Lord, DeVader, and Alliger, 1986). Researchers have found that an understanding of implicit theories of leadership is important because people seem to use their implicit theories, in terms of automatically guiding their actions, or when asked to judge a leader's performance.

Similarly, people also hold assumptions about how followers should respond to the orders of an authority figure. As I mentioned, people in Western cultures like the United States are socialized to feel obligated to obey the orders of a legitimate agent of authority. Moreover, they often expect others to do likewise. For example, H.C. Kelman and V.L. Hamilton sampled U.S. citizens' opinions toward the obedient and destructive actions of the soldiers under Lieutenant Calley's command after the My Lai massacre in Vietnam. A large majority of respondents reported that they would have also followed orders to shoot innocent civilians if such orders came from a commanding officer. They also reported that they would expect that most other people would feel and do the same.

At the same time, people in Western societies like the United States also like to maintain a sense of individualism in their self-concepts. In other words, there is a tendency for people to like to see themselves as autonomous decision makers, unique and independent from the group and the social environment. For this reason, I find that it is common for many students to frown upon others they perceive as blindly obeying the orders of an authority figure, particularly an authority figure that is not perceived to be illegitimate or destructive.

Deciding whether an authority figure is legitimate or not, is however a complex social process, and there may be a great deal of variability between subordinates' decisions. One method I use to begin a discussion among students on this issue is to replicate a simple sociological study by F.H. Sanford.

Sanford used a projective cartoon in an attempt to sample people's attitudes toward being led. Although the procedure has some methodological flaws, I have found it useful to stimulate a class discussion about why people may or may not obey orders. As Sanford did in his study, I hand out in class a cartoon drawing of a dozen men and women standing close together in a group. All the group members are facing in the direction of a male figure, standing a short distance apart from the group. The male figure is pictured facing back toward the group. Drawn above his head is a cartoon balloon with the following caption typed within it: "Since I'm head of this group you'd better do as I say." Pictured over the heads of the group members in the middle of the pack, is drawn an empty cartoon balloon. I ask students to read the caption from the lone male figure and then write down what they think that person in the group will say in response to the other's statement. I then collect the sheets, tabulate the responses, and summarize the findings across several classes. These results are then presented and discussed with students during the next class meeting. Interestingly, I usually find similar results to those found by Sanford in 1948. Approximately 10–12 percent of students believe the person in the group would give an accepting response to the leader (e.g., "Okay, I'll do it"). Approximately 12–15 percent usually give some form of tentative acceptance, for example, "I need more information first," or "Maybe, it depends what you want." Ten to 12 percent give what Sanford categorized as a group centered response: "Let us all vote on it," or "We should all decide together." Ten to 15 percent fall into the miscellaneous or don't know type of response. Finally, the majority of responses, approximately 50–60 percent of students believes most people would give a rejecting response (e.g., "Forget it," or "Go to hell"). I find this exercise useful to begin a discussion because many students are surprised to find that other people don't share their views. I point out to students that the tendency to feel that most other people hold similar attitudes to one's own is known by social psychologists as the false-consensus effect.

Students giving non-accepting responses are generally surprised that anyone would feel obligated to conform to the demands of a "self-appointed" leader. In contrast, students who give accepting responses point out that the cartoon lacks a great deal of detail or information. These students argue that it doesn't seem unreasonable to obey the person's orders. I then ask students to discuss whether they think the differences in students' opinions was due to differences in stable personality traits, or due to students focusing on different aspects of the situation represented in the cartoon?

At the end of this open discussion, I assign several short writing assignments focusing on the following questions: What function does obedience to authority serve society? Under what conditions would we expect a person to obey or disobey an authority figure and how are people perceived by others when they do obey or disobey? What factors play a role in deciding when someone will or will not obey a command they feel is morally or ethically wrong? Students are then assigned Milgram's 1974 text *Obedience to Authority* and we begin to take up discussion of Milgram's work.

Although Stanley Milgram's studies of obedience to authority are well known among students of social psychology, many students in leadership studies programs seem unaware about the relevance and importance of his work. I believe it is important for students in leadership studies programs to understand Milgram's work for the following reasons.

First, many students have been exposed to popular books about leadership that I believe overemphasize a dispositional approach (i.e., traits and internal characteristics) when discussing successful and influential leaders. Social and situational variables are often overlooked or minimized by the authors of these texts when describing successful leaders.

Milgram's work also illustrates how a person living in a complex society is exposed to opposing social forces. For instance, Milgram's subjects experienced a conflict between the moral obligation not to harm an innocent person versus the normative demands to obey an authority figure. Milgram's work is an excellent way to have students engage in a self-examination of their own implicit theories about authority and leader-follower relationships. Human beings often act in an automatic or mindless way, and we use our implicit theories, stereotypes, and other social assumptions as guides for our behavior. While at times, our assumptions about others can lead to correct behavior and inferences, they are nevertheless not always accurate, nor are they always good *predictors* of what other people will do in the future. Hence we cannot always rely on our implicit theory that "good people will not follow bad leaders." Milgram's findings will show us that a social situation can corrupt even good people into doing harmful things.

Finally, Milgram's work is a reminder that as citizens of a democracy we are not immune to destructive obedience and thus, we need to be constantly on guard. Milgram believed his findings "raise the possibility that human nature or, more specifically, the kind of character produced in American democratic society cannot be counted on to insulate its citizens from brutality and inhuman treatment at the direction of malevolent authority" (189). I found it interesting that Milgram was once asked why, as he had originally planned to do, he didn't conduct his experiment in post-war Germany in order to compare levels of obedience with U.S. citizens. His reply was that he never saw the need to because he had already found so much obedience in America (quoted in Meyer 73).

Milgram would typically bring a subject into the laboratory at Yale University and inform him that he was to be part of a scientific experiment on human learning. The subject would then be introduced to an "experimenter," who was actually a confederate hired by Milgram. This role was played by a thirty-one-year-old high school biology teacher dressed in a gray technician's lab coat. The subject was assigned, by a rigged drawing, to the role of "teacher" and given the duty of delivering electric shocks to another "subject," assigned the role of "learner." In actuality, the learner was not another subject but a forty-seven-year-old (mild-mannered looking) accountant, trained to act out the role of the victim.

The subject (i.e., teacher) was told he would read aloud a list of word pairs, for example, wild-duck, blue-box, nice-day and so on down a long list. After finishing the list, the subject was to announce an item from the previously read list, for example, "blue." The subject would then read several possible responses, one of which was previously paired with the item on the original list, for example, "sky, ink, box, lamp." The learner, sitting in another room, was to press a button if he believed that "sky" was the word originally paired with "blue."

The subject, sitting in an adjacent room, would see a light on a panel in front of him go on, which informed him of the learner's choice. The subject was then informed that he would be giving the learner a 15-volt shock for his first incorrect response and would then be increasing the level of punishment by 15-volt increments for every subsequent incorrect answer the learner gave. The subject then witnessed the learner being strapped into a chair and watched as electrode paste and electrodes were attached to the left forearm of the learner. The experimenter then announced to both subject and learner that the paste was to avoid blistering, and that although the shocks would be painful, they would not cause any permanent tissue damage. The subject was then seated in an adjacent room and shown a large instrument box that would be used to deliver the punishment to the learner.

The instrument panel of the "shock generator" consisted of 30 switches set in a horizontal line. The thirty switches were marked from 15 to 450 volts in 15-volt increments. Below the range of voltage labels were printed written designations: Slight Shock, Moderate Shock, Strong Shock, Very Strong Shock, Intense Shock, Extremely Intense Shock, Danger Severe Shock, and finally the last two switches were simply marked XXX. Each time the subject depressed a switch on the shock generator a corresponding small red light came on over the switch, a voltage meter arrow on the face of the box swung to the far right side, an internal relay gave off a clicking sound and an electric buzzing sound was emitted. The subject was also instructed to shout out the current voltage level prior to administering each shock.

Prior to the beginning of the experiment, the third switch on the shock generator (45 volts) was depressed and an actual 45-volt shock was administered to the wrist of the subject. This was done to increase the subject's belief about the authenticity of the study. Although no shocks were ever actually administered to the "learner" during the experiment, he was trained to make a predetermined set of errors and to respond in a specific manner.

Although Milgram, who was surprised by his findings, later conducted intensive and careful debriefing sessions with his subjects, his work raised considerable debate among social psychologists over the ethical treatment of human subjects (see Baumrind and Forsyth).

The main measure of interest to Milgram was the maximum level of shock a subject would administer to the learner before refusing to obey the authority of the experimenter, what Milgram called the break off point. If subjects hesitated in delivering the shock, the experimenter was trained to avoid giving threats or rewards for obedience, and was instead trained to give several verbal "prods" to the subject in the following sequence, if necessary: "Please continue. The experiment requires that you continue. It is absolutely essential that you continue. You have no other choice, you must go on."

If the subject asked the experimenter about any permanent physical injury to the learner, the experimenter replied, "Although the shocks may be painful, there is no permanent tissue damage, so please go on." The experimenter would then follow with prods #2-4 if necessary. If the subject implied that the "learner" didn't want to continue, the experimenter would reply: "Whether the learner likes it or not, you must go on until he has learned all the word pairs correctly. So please go on." If needed, the experimenter would then use prods #2-4. Finally, if the learner refused to answer at all, which he was trained to do at higher levels of punishment, the experimenter was trained to tell the subject that he must treat a non-response as an incorrect response and continue administering increasingly higher levels of shock.

Now imagine for a moment that you are a subject in Milgram's experiment. The experiment appears to be an important scientific study and the experimenter seems very knowledgeable and credible. In essence, the experimenter appears to you to be a legitimate authority figure. After hearing an overview of the study, you agree to participate and apparently, by chance, you have been assigned to be the "teacher." Your role as teacher is then patiently and politely explained to you by the experimenter. You then receive a sample shock from the shock generator. The shock you received isn't pleasant, but by now you are convinced this is an important and "real scientific study."

The experiment begins with the learner giving correct responses. After several minutes, however, you are surprised when the learner makes his first error. You look down at the first of many tiny switches. As instructed, you announce in a loud voice that the shock level is set at 15 volts. You press down the first switch and you hear an internal relay click, you see the voltage meter on the shock generator box swing to the right, you hear a buzzing sound.

You just administered a mild 15-volt shock to the learner. However, it appears to have had no harmful effect. A few minutes later more errors occur, and you throw the appropriate switches. So far the shocks appear mild. The experiment continues uneventfully, until the learner makes a mistake at the 75-volt level. You once again announce the shock level, press down the appropriate switch, there is a click, a buzz, but this time you hear a grunt of pain from the learner in the next room. The learner makes more mistakes, there are more groans of pain, and you are surprised to look down at the switches and find that you have now moved along into the middle of the line of switches. As the voltage level increases, you hear louder and more agonizing grunts of pain from the learner. You are now very distressed and you turn to the experimenter and ask if the learner is all right. The experimenter responds to your inquiry in a polite but a firm manner, telling you to please go on. If necessary, the experimenter uses the other verbal "prods."

You are becoming increasingly distressed as the experiment continues, you know it isn't right to do this to the learner. At 150 volts, the learner screams that he wants out of the chair, and that he doesn't want to be part of the experiment. You hesitate, but the experimenter, sitting calmly behind you, informs you in a pleasant, but firm voice that you must continue. At this point, you are very upset and disturbed by the experiment. It is obvious to you that the shocks are now extremely painful to the learner and he is no longer a willing participant in the study. You keep thinking the experimenter will end the session, because each shock is now producing a loud and sharp cry of pain from the learner.

At 270 volts you hear loud screams and the learner pounds on the wall and shouts that he can't take it. You hesitate again telling the experimenter that the session has got to stop. The experimenter again tells you that you must continue and finish the experiment. You are perspiring and your heart is pounding. The experimenter instructs you to continue to the next shock level. You keep hoping the learner will not make any more errors, so you focus your attention on reading the list of words as carefully and distinctly as you possibly can.

At 300 volts, the learner screams in pain and shouts that he refuses to give any more responses. Shaken you turn to the experimenter, he calmly and firmly informs you that you must treat a non-response as an incorrect response and you should administer the shock. In distress, you ask the experimenter, "Who is going to be responsible for this?" The experimenter calmly answers that he will be responsible.

Reluctantly, you announce the level of shock to be delivered and flip down the tiny switch. Click, buzz. This time you don't hear a response from the learner, in fact, you never hear another noise from the learner again. You ask the experimenter if someone needs to go check in on the learner.

The experimenter tells you that the shocks will not cause any permanent damage and that the experiment must continue to the end. You protest, telling the experimenter that there are too many words left on the list to continue and you are now near the very end of the row of switches. The experimenter instructs you to use the last (XXX) switch, labeled 450 volts for all subsequent mistakes or non-responses. You reluctantly once again read the next set of words, but the learner doesn't give any type of response.

Would you throw the last switch?

If you are like most people, you want to believe that you would never have obeyed the experimenter's last demands, and you certainly would have disobeyed after the first few mild shocks were delivered to the learner. Moreover, you believe that since you would have disobeyed, other "normal" people like you would have also disobeyed the experimenter.

Just as Milgram did with his students, I ask my students to predict what percentage of people would obey the experimenter and go all the way to 450 volts. Like Milgram, I am always intrigued that my students consistently underestimate the level of obedience found by Milgram. Most students usually predict less than 10 percent of subjects would fully obey the experimenter's orders. Milgram also asked a sample of psychiatrists, behavioral scientists, and psychology graduate students to make a prediction about the level of obedience. These professionals tended to predict no more than 2 to 3 percent of subjects would give Milgram full obedience. Many of them based their estimates on the percentage of subjects who, in a random sample might be expected to show sadistic tendencies or other similar symptoms of mental disorders. Milgram's findings were surprising, even to him, because they were very different from anyone's predictions.

Milgram found that 65 percent, or 26 out of 40 subjects in his first experiment fully obeyed the experimenter and delivered an XXX-450 volt shock to the learner.

My leadership study students, like most people, apply a disposition interpretation to Milgram's findings. In other words, they focus on the personalities of Milgram's subjects, and give little weight to situational factors. Again, social psychologists refer to this tendency as the fundamental attribution error.

The "fundamental attribution error" is the tendency of people to overestimate the influence of internal personality traits and underestimate the roles that social-situational factors play in determining another's behavior. Of course, I can't blame my students, because researchers have found that it is quite common for the fundamental attribution error to come into play when interpreting Milgram's findings (as the work of Miller, Gillen, Schenker, and Radlove suggests). Furthermore, it is difficult to get people *not* to form negative impressions of Milgram's subjects. People have a tendency to believe in a just and predictable world in which good people do good things, and only bad people do bad things.

I spend a great deal of time discussing both the fundamental attribution error with students and the power of situational forces that influenced Milgram's subjects, because researchers have shown that watching video-reenactment or even role-playing the parts in Milgram's experiment may not be enough to persuade students to focus on situational influences (Bierbrauer 1979).

My students tend to view Milgram's subjects as more immoral, heartless, unintelligent, or simply evil compared to themselves or their friends. As I mentioned, I often find leadership studies students susceptible to the fundamental attribution error. Although I am speculating, I believe it is because many of them have been exposed to popular leadership texts that often give anecdotal accounts of successful leaders. These accounts often over emphasize the dispositional qualities and traits of the leader (e.g., interpersonal style, vision, aggressiveness) without discussing the social and situational forces that were also influential in determining the leader's success.

One of the most common questions I receive from students is "How did the personalities of obedient subjects differ from that of non-obedient subjects?"

Recall that almost all of Milgram's subjects gave the learner an intense shock before breaking off, and 65 percent of subjects fully obeyed, and yet, what about the 35 percent of subjects who did not fully obey? Do these subjects have measurable differences in their personalities that might help us explain Milgram's findings, and if so, to what extent did these differences determine the subjects' behavior?

To psychologists, the term "personality" usually refers to a unique and relatively consistent pattern of behavior. If you look at Milgram's subjects, however, you will not find a consistent pattern of obedience or non-obedience. Moreover, when Milgram looked for various other personality differences between subjects that obeyed and disobeyed he found no significant differences, and concluded that the dispositions of his subjects did not appear to play a significant role in determining his findings (Elms and Milgram 1966).

Subsequent research has found a slight tendency for people of lower social-economic status, and people with less education to be more obedient to authority figures. Other variables that have been found by some researchers to be positively associated with greater levels of obedience are religiosity and authoritarianism. Unfortunately, the findings from research with these variables are not very strong, nor entirely consistent across different studies.

Because students assume that personality *should* play a major role in destructive obedience, I believe it is important to discuss with students why one's personality may not always predict one's actions.

Many social psychologists take an interactional perspective toward personality and social behavior. This perspective assumes that the variability in a person's behavior is often due to the interaction between internal dispositions (e.g., stable traits) and situational factors present in the specific setting (see Snyder and Ickes). Under other conditions, behavior may be determined more by internal dispositional traits (i.e., weak situations), or by the social-situational factors within the context of the environment (strong situations). Situations are said to be psychologically "strong" or "weak" depending on the aspects of the situation that shift the cause of a person's behavior from a situational locus to a dispositional one, or vice versa. From the perspective of the individual, a weak situation or experimental setting, is one in which there are relatively few salient cues to guide one's behavior. Because the situation is relatively unstructured and ambiguous, the dispositional traits of an individual play a relatively larger role in determining behavior. If these personality traits can be measured accurately they may also be relatively good predictors of a person's actual behavior.

In contrast, psychologically strong situations shift the locus of causality from being dispositional in nature toward being more situational. Psychologically strong situations are perceived by the individual as having many salient behavioral cues that provide social structure and guidance about how to act. Under these conditions social-situational variables may dominate over dispositional traits in guiding, and in predicting behavior.

The situation that faced Milgram's subjects was actually more complex than many students realize it to be. For example, Milgram believed that humans can function autonomously, or through the assumption of roles, submerge themselves into a larger hierarchical social system. Yet, because of this capacity to function both independently and as a part of a larger social system, we often experience tension or anxiety, what Milgram called "strain." As Milgram stated, "the very fact of dual capacities requires a design compromise. We are not perfectly tailored for complete autonomy, nor for total submission" (1974, 153).

Milgram's subjects faced a great deal of strain because they were faced with a difficult dilemma: on the one hand, they had been socialized to obey a legitimate authority figure; on the other, each subject was faced with violating his own personal moral and ethical standards against harming another individual.

Milgram also believed that human beings have developed several mechanisms to reduce strain. In the case of Milgram's subjects, if the strain became too great, subjects could reduce it by eventually disobeying the experimenter, as some did. Yet, there were also several powerful, although seemingly invisible, social forces at work to reduce strain and keep subjects obeying the experimenter. To understand these powerful social forces, Milgram conducted a series of systematic experiments, similar to his original paradigm, except each focused on a different aspect of the social situation.

In one study, Milgram manipulated the physical proximity of the subject to the learner. When the subject moved closer to the learner while administering shocks (i.e., the same room), obedience among subjects declined from 63 percent to 40 percent. As physical distance between the subject and learner decreased even more—for example, subjects had to physically hold the learner's hand onto the shock pad—the level of full obedience decreased to 30 percent.

The physical distance between the subject and the authority figure also influenced obedience. As the experimenter physically moved away from the subject, for example, gave commands over a telephone from another room, the level of full obedience among subjects decreased to 21 percent.

Some critics of Milgram's original study argued it was a fluke, due to the prestige and power attributed to the experimental location, in this case Yale University. To test this assumption, Milgram moved his experiment to a run down, empty storefront building, in Bridgeport, Connecticut. Although obedience declined somewhat to 48 percent, it was still very high. Subsequent cross-cultural replications of Milgram's work also showed remarkable similarity to Milgram's original findings, with only minor variations in levels of obedience between different countries (Kilham and Mann 1974; Shanab and Yahya 1977).

Milgram found that the subjects would not obey someone they did not perceive to be a legitimate authority figure, for example, a confederate playing the part of another subject who happened to be present during the experiment.

Milgram found that the influence of the authority figure was significantly decreased by the presence of a disobedient role model. When subjects were placed with two other teachers, actually confederates, who defied the experimenter, 90 percent of subjects disobeyed when instructed to continue.

Milgram found that subjects often perceived themselves to be a tool of the experimenter and thus attributed responsibility for their actions to the experimenter. Other researchers have found that assigning personal responsibility to subjects for any harm coming to the learner results in most subjects terminating the experiment as soon as the learner expresses any discomfort (see, for example, Tilker).

Some critics questioned the generalizabilty of Milgram's findings, arguing his experiment created an artificial situation in which subjects obeyed because they never believed the shocks would cause any real harm to the learners. Other empirical research, however, has supported Milgram's original work.

For example, in an interesting set of studies, investigators from the Netherlands simulated Milgram's experiments, but instead of having subjects administer physical violence, they had subjects administer more common and real types of harm.

In an experiment involving an elaborate cover story, subjects were led to believe that they would be an interview administrator, conducting an important job interview with a well-qualified job candidate (actually a confederate of the experiment) who desperately needs the job. The subject is ordered by the experimenter to make 15 scripted and increasingly demeaning remarks to the candidate during his interview. During the interview it becomes clear to subjects that the remarks are increasing the candidate's stress level and decreasing his performance and his opportunity to secure a needed job. Similar to the Milgram study, the candidate repeatedly asked the subject to stop interrupting him and let him continue with his answers.

The researchers measured the number of subjects who would disobey the experimenter and break off from reading the list of stress-inducing remarks. Although subjects knew that they were destroying the chances of a well-qualified person receiving a job that person desperately needed, 22 of 24 subjects obeyed the experimenter and read all 15 statements, in spite of the candidate's repeated requests to desist. On average, subjects made 14.4 out of 15 possible harmful remarks.

Another variation of this study used personnel managers as subjects. The researchers expected that the training and professional experience of personnel managers would allow them to resist the unethical commands of the experimenter. This was not the case. Almost all the personnel managers fully obeyed, and the one who did finally resist nonetheless made 11 of the 15 stress-inducing remarks.

As in Milgram's study, follow up questionnaires and interviews revealed that subjects in the Netherlands research did not have an easy time obeying orders. Subjects reported that they were well aware they were harming the job candidate and they experienced a great deal of stress from doing so. They also reported that they felt the experimenter was being unfair, and irresponsible, yet they reported respecting him. Finally, as in Milgram's experiment, subjects felt it was the experimenter that was responsible for any harm done to the job candidate. They felt no personal responsibility (Meeus and Raaijmakers 1986).

For ethical reasons, psychologists today would not be allowed to replicate Milgram's experiment because we know how stressful it was for subjects. The empirical evidence we do have from related studies supports Milgram's findings and many of his conclusions.

Milgram offered a comprehensive analysis and theory for destructive obedience, however, I will only focus on his conclusions that I use in relation to my own leadership studies courses. What follows is a description of several important psychological concepts that I present and discuss in my courses.

Milgram believed that once a subject agreed to participate in the experiment he or she entered into an agentic state. In other words, instead of perceiving himself or herself as an autonomous decision maker, the subject shifts toward viewing himself or herself as a tool of the authority. In a sense, as the situation becomes more socially structured (i.e., a strong situation) that may change the way a subject perceives and processes information. As Milgram described it, "The subject comes to view himself as an agent for executing the wishes of another person. Once an individual conceives his action in this light, profound alterations occur in his behavior and his internal functioning" (1974, 133).

To reduce their anxiety, many subjects appeared to refocus their attention away from the learner and onto the technical or mechanical aspects of their task. For example, Milgram noticed that many subjects seemed overly concerned with how well they were flipping the switches or how clearly they were reading the list of word pairs. By focusing on "their job" subjects seemed to relinquish their responsibility onto the experimenter and reduce their distress.

Often students, and colleagues of mine suggest that subjects who obeyed Milgram lacked a "moral compass," that would enable them to distinguish right from wrong. I would argue that these subjects had a working moral compass; unfortunately, the power of the social situation in Milgram's experiment realigned it with that of the experimenter and away from the suffering of the learner. By aligning themselves with the experimenter and not the learner, doing "good" for subjects became synonymous with meeting the expectations of the experimenter and not the needs of the learner.

Milgram also found that after delivering several shocks, there was a tendency for subjects to devalue the learner (e.g., he is stubborn and stupid) as a possible means of justifying their actions.

Milgram felt that there were several social norms that served to bind subjects to the experimenter, hindering them from breaking off, although they may have desired to do so. For example, it becomes awkward to withdraw from the experiment after having made a public commitment to participate and after being "fairly" designated the teacher.

The experimenter is also perceived by subjects as a "scientist," a position given high status and credibility in our society. Moreover, the experimenter maintained an air of moral aloofness throughout the experiment. He was always firm but polite to subjects, never personally threatening them. The experimenter's manner and verbal "prods" seemed to imply a moral obligation to continue the experiment that went beyond the individual needs of the subject. Thus, many subjects reported that they felt embarrassed to tell the experimenter they wanted to quit because they were personally feeling uncomfortable about what they were doing. In other words, their personal discomfort had to take a back seat to the greater goals of science. In contrast to anthropomorphism (attributing human characteristics to nonhuman things), Milgram coined the term "counteranthropomorphism" to describe this process.

Counteranthropomorphism is the tendency for his subjects to deny any human element or human agency behind his experiment. For example, in post-experimental interviews, many subjects reported feeling they had to go on with the study for the good of the experiment, or for the good of science. Milgram summed up the subjects' reactions in the following way, "He does not ask the seemingly obvious question, whose experiment? Why should the designer be served while the victim suffers? The wishes of a man, the designer of the experiment, have become part of a schema which exerts in the subject's mind a force that transcends the personal. The experiment acquired an impersonal momentum of its own" (1974, 9). Although all of Milgram's subjects gave intense shocks and many gave potentially lethal shocks, the experiment had a very benign and placid beginning. By the time subjects became uncomfortable with their actions they had already obeyed and flipped several switches. The gradual increase in shock intensity proved to be a slippery slope for many subjects, a "slippery slope from the innocent to the evil" (Sabini, 49).

One of the most difficult findings for students to grasp is that subjects often acted in a manner that seemed in direct opposition to their beliefs and values. For instance, in post-experimental interviews, subjects often reported that they were well aware that what they were doing was terribly wrong, and they felt terrible about doing it, yet they could not bring themselves to disobey the experimenter. While social psychologists are aware that attitudes, intentions, and values do not always result in corresponding actions, it is often unsettling to students. This is disturbing to students because there is a tendency for people in our society to believe that the world is a just and predictable place, a place where one should be able to predict that other people's actions are consistent with their beliefs. However, our internally held moral beliefs are not the only factors working to influence our behavior. Milgram's research shows us that his subjects' moral codes could be "shunted aside with relative ease by a calculated restructuring of the informational and social field" (1974, 7).

Once Milgram's subjects enter into the agentic state and become a tool of the experimenter, they become very willing to give up varying degrees of responsibility to the experimenter. Yet, even more disturbing to Milgram was the tendency for destructive obedience to significantly increase when subjects were in the presence of other obedient "teachers" or when subjects simply conveyed the experimenter's orders to other teachers. Being a single link in a chain appears to allow people to significantly relinquish much of their personal responsibility. Milgram feared that in our ever increasingly complex society, where individuals tend to work on specific and narrowly focused tasks, that eventually no one person would be left to assume responsibility for any destructive action.

Milgram's work is disturbing, but I believe important for anyone wishing to study an important aspect of leadership. We must remember that Milgram's research does not simply demonstrate that people obey authority, but shows us how influential and powerful social situations can be in determining the actions of people. Furthermore, his work challenges our implicit notion concerning why people obey destructive commands, emphasizing the fact that situational forces play a larger role than most people expect. We can also not assume that one's personality, character, or moral upbringing will inoculate one from destructive obedience.

I have found that having students reconsider their own implicit theories, biases, and assumptions concerning obedience can result in more mindful types of discussions and I believe significantly enhance their understanding, and appreciation of Milgram's work. Milgram's research is disturbing, demonstrating that social forces can make even good people do terrible things, however, his work and that of others has also shown what conditions can be altered in a situation in an attempt to reduce destructive obedience. For example, exposure to disobedient models, increasing social support from others, providing evidence that an authority figure is pursuing selfish goals, assigning personal responsibility for outcomes, increasing empathy, and increasing the physical and psychological proximity to the victim are all conditions that tend to reduce levels of destructive obedience. I often ask students to write or discuss ways these factors can be used in group or organizational settings to reduce the chances of destructive obedience occurring.

As students read and learn about the effective and influential characteristics of leaders, I ask that they also focus their attention and efforts on understanding the less visible and often more complex social and situational factors that may be exerting a powerful influence on the behavior of both leaders and followers. In my opinion, there seems to be a growing interest in our society to find leaders with strong and influential personalities that will rescue us from our troubles. I caution students that we also must devote an equal amount of effort and energy to understanding the structure of our social environments, because as Milgram argued, "Often, it is not so much the kind of person a man is as the kind of situation in which he finds himself that determines how he will act" (1992, 155).

Works Cited

Baumrind, D. "Some Thoughts on the Ethics of Research: After Reading Milgram's 'Behavioral Study of Obedience'." *American Psychologist* 19 (1964): 421–423.

Bierbrauer, G. "Why Did He Do It? Attributions of Obedience and the Phenomenon of Dispositional Bias." *European Journal of Social Psychology* 9 (1979): 67–84.

Elms, A. C., and S. Milgram. "Personality Characteristics Associated with Obedience and Defiance Toward Authoritative Command." *Journal of Experimental Research in Personality* 1 (1966): 282–289.

Forsyth, D. R. "Moral Judgement: The Influence of Ethical Ideology." *Personality and Social Psychology Bulletin* 7 (1981): 218–223.

———. *Our Social World*. Pacific Grove, CA: Brooks/Cole, 1995.

Kelman, H. C., and V. L. Hamilton. *Crimes of Obedience*. New Haven, CT: Yale University Press, 1989.

Kilham, W., and L. Mann. "Level of Destructive Obedience as a Function of Transmitter and Executant Roles in the Milgram Obedience Paradigm." *Journal of Personality and Social Psychology* 29 (1974): 696–702.

Lord, R. G., C. L. DeVader, and G. M. Alliger. "A Meta-analysis of the Relation Between Personality Traits and Leadership Perceptions: An Application of Validity Generalization Procedures." *Journal of Applied Psychology* 71 (1986): 402–410.

Meeus, W. H. J., and Q. A. W. Raaijmakers. "Administrative Obedience: Carrying Out Orders to Use Psychological Administrative Violence." *European Journal of Social Psychology* 16 (1986): 311–324.

Meyer, P. "If Hitler Asked You to Electrocute a Stranger, Would You? Probably." *Esquire Magazine* (1970): 73.

Milgram, S. *Obedience to Authority*. New York: Harper & Row, 1974.

———. "Some Conditions of Obedience and Disobedience to Authority." In *The Individual in the Social World: Essays and Experiments*, ed. M. Silver and S. Milgram eds. New York: McGraw Hill, 1992.

Miller, A. G., B. Gillen, C. Schenker, and S. Radlove. "The Prediction and Perception of Obedience to Authority." *Journal of Personality* 42 (1974): 23–42.

Ross, L. "The Intuitive Psychologist and His Shortcomings: Distortions in the Attribution Process." In *Advance in Experimental Social Psychology*, ed. L. Berkowitz. New York: Academic Press, 1977. 10: 173–220.

Sabini, J. *Social psychology*. New York: W. W. Norton, 1995.

Sabini, J., and M. Silver. *Moralities of Everyday Life*. New York: Norton, 1982.

Sanford, F. H. "The Follower's Role in Leadership Phenomena." In *Readings in Social Psychology*, The Committee on the Teaching of Social Psychology of the Society for the Psychological Study of Social Issues. New York: Henry Holt, 1952.

Shanab, M. E., and K. A. Yahya. "A Behavioral Study of Obedience in Children." *Journal of Personality and Social Psychology* 35 (1977): 530–536.

Snyder, M., and W. Ickes. "Personality and Social Behavior." In *Handbook of Social Psychology*. 3e. ed. G. Lindzey and E. Aronson. New York: Random House, 1985.

Tilker, H. A. "Socially Responsible Behavior as a Function of Observer Responsibility and Victim Feedback." *Journal of Personality and Social Psychology* 14 (1970): 95–100.

7

Earl Warren, Thurgood Marshall, *Brown v. Board of Education of Topeka*: Portraits in Leadership

Thomas D. Cavenagh

This essay traces the paths of two individuals that converged in an era of tumultuous social change and unrest to move the nation toward the racial integration of public schools. Earl Warren and Thurgood Marshall are responsible for the United States Supreme Court cases known as *Brown v. Board of Education* I and II that required the desegregation of public schools throughout the country. Warren possessed an important leadership ability in his skill at forging consensus among a deeply divided United States Supreme Court. Marshall demonstrated his own leadership skill in his capability to overcome the ambivalence of his civil rights followers through tireless advocacy. Both possessed, as well, a fundamental quality of good leadership: a profound commitment to the primacy of principle.

To begin this essay, I will present an overview of the *Brown* decisions, drawing on the language of the opinions as well as the social and legal circumstances out of which the decisions came. Next, I will portray Earl Warren as the architect of the *Brown* decisions and as the leader of the United States Supreme Court during his tenure. Finally, I will describe Thurgood Marshall as the force which brought the *Brown* case to the Court in a posture which compelled the Court to rule in his favor.

The Brown Decision

"Oyez! Oyez! Oyez! All persons having business before the honorable, the Supreme Court of the United States, are invited to draw near and give their attention, for the Court is now sitting. God save the United States and this Honorable Court."

With these grand words, argument commenced in the United States Supreme Court in the case of *Brown v. Board of Education* (347 U.S. 483 1954). *Brown* was argued as a class action lawsuit by Thurgood Marshall, among others, of the Legal Defense and Educational Fund, Inc. of the National Association for the Advancement of Colored People on behalf of minority plaintiffs seeking admission to the public schools in several states, including Kansas, on a nonsegregated basis. Each of the defendant states had laws permitting or requiring segregated public schools. The case was initially argued to the Court on December 9, 1952, following extensive litigation first at the state, and then the lower federal court levels. At the request of the Court, additional argument was made on December 8, 1953. This second presentation was due in part to the death of Chief Justice Fred Vinson and his replacement as Chief Justice by Earl Warren, and also in part to the Court's need for further argument on the importance to the present case of the circumstances surrounding the adoption of the Fourteenth Amendment in 1868.

The Court issued a stunning, unanimous opinion in favor of Brown and the other plaintiffs, authored by Warren, on May 17, 1954. In that opinion, the Court held that public schools which are segregated on the basis of race violate the Equal Protection Clause of the Fourteenth Amendment to the United States Constitution[1] even where they offer measurably equal physical educational facilities, such as buildings, grounds, and classroom resources, because such schools deprive excluded minority children of equal learning and development opportunities. The opinion focused solely on the constitutional merits of the case and did not describe a course of action for changing the segregated schools of which the plaintiffs complained. Instead, the Court ordered the parties to deliver further argument on a precise desegregation method for the Court to impose on states where segregated schools existed.

On April 11 through 14, 1955, the Court heard argument, again from Thurgood Marshall, among others, on the formulation of a suitable decree from the Court which would spell out an acceptable plan of action for desegregation. The Court issued a second unanimous opinion (349 U.S. 294 1955) on May 31, 1955, again authored by Chief Justice Warren. In that opinion, the Court authorized state and lower federal courts to review local desegregation plans. In addition, the Court empowered the local courts to compel recalcitrant legislators to create such plans should they refuse to do so. In the opinion, the Court also returned to and reinforced its ruling in the initial opinion that all federal, state, and local laws which create conditions of segregation are unconstitutional and must be repealed and replaced with desegregation plans.[2]

The two *Brown* decisions had the effect of overruling the infamous *Plessy v. Ferguson* case (163 U.S. 537 1896). The Court held in *Plessy* that a state law requiring racially segregated, but equal, rail car accommodations, and punishing a passenger with fines or imprisonment for insisting on anything else, did not violate the antebellum Thirteenth Amendment, which prohibits slavery and involuntary servitude, or the Fourteenth Amendment,[3] which ensures equal protection under the laws. The passing of the nearly unanimous *Plessy* Court supported the host of public facilities segregation regulations known as "Jim Crow" laws.

The *Plessy* Court considered an 1890 Louisiana law which provided with respect to interstate travel that

> ... all railway companies carrying passengers in their coaches in this state, shall provide equal but separate accommodations for the White, and colored races, by providing two or more passenger coaches for each passenger train, or by dividing the passenger coaches by partition so as to secure separate accommodations ... No person or persons shall be permitted to occupy seats in coaches other than the ones assigned to them, on account of the race they belong to. (540)

Plessy, who was "seven-eighths Caucasian and one-eighth African blood," and in whom "the mixture of blood was not discernible" purchased a ticket for a journey which would start and end in Louisiana; the Louisiana law applied to trips of this nature only. He did so specifically to test the constitutionality of the Louisiana law and more broadly the Jim Crow laws. Consistent with the Louisiana law, Plessy was ordered by a conductor to vacate a "white race only" passenger car and be seated in the separate "black only" passenger car. When he refused he was forcibly removed and imprisoned pending trial.

The Court held that it was "too clear for argument" (542) that the Louisiana law did not conflict with the Thirteenth amendment, agreeing with previous decisions that

> the act of a mere individual, the owner of an inn, a public conveyance or place of amusement, refusing accommodations to colored people, cannot be justly regarded as imposing any badge of slavery or servitude upon the applicant, but only as involving an ordinary civil injury, properly cognizable by the laws of the state, and presumably subject to redress by those laws until the contrary appears. (542, 3)

The Court read the Constitution narrowly, defining slavery and involuntary servitude as states of bondage, the ownership of mankind as chattel or the control of the labor and services of one man for the benefit of another, and found that the Louisiana law did not place Plessy into a position consistent with these definitions. The Court held that a distinction between people, even one founded purely upon race, did not necessarily destroy the legal equality of either race or tend to reestablish slavery. Indeed, the Court expressed uncertainty on the question of why Plessy invoked the Thirteenth Amendment at all.

Perhaps the more significant component of the Court's decision was its refusal to apply the Fourteenth Amendment in Plessy's favor. The Court traced the history of the judicial interpretation of the Fourteenth Amendment citing cases supporting the prohibition of interracial marriage and, significantly, the establishment of "separate schools for white and colored children" (544). The Court concluded that the purpose of the Fourteenth Amendment

> ... was undoubtedly to enforce the absolute equality of the two races before the law, but in the nature of things, it could not have been intended to abolish distinctions based upon color, or to enforce social, as distinguished from political, equality, or a commingling of the two races upon terms unsatisfactory to either. Laws permitting, and even requiring, their separation, in places where they are liable to be brought into contact, do not necessarily imply the inferiority of either race to the other, and have been generally, if not universally, recognized as within the competency of the state legislatures in the exercise of their police power. (544)

The Court made much of the distinction between political rights and social rights believing the former to be the object of the protection of the Fourteenth Amendment and the latter to be largely unprotected. The Court was, as a result, unoffended by Jim Crow type regulations, but willing to nullify laws limiting, for example, service on juries to whites only, believing that such laws when applied to minorities constituted a "step towards reducing them to a condition of servility" (545). This narrow reading of the Constitution led the Court to hold that Plessy's argument that he had a property right in his reputation, which was abridged by his separation, was not persuasive because

> If he be a white man, and assigned to the colored coach, he may have his action for damages against the company for being deprived of his so-called property. Upon the other hand, if he be a colored man, and be so assigned, he has been deprived of no property, since he is not lawfully entitled to the reputation of being a white man. (549)

The Court concluded:

> We consider the underlying fallacy of the plaintiff's argument to consist in the assumption that the enforced separation of the two races stamps the colored race with a badge of inferiority. If this be so, it is not by reason of anything found in the act, but solely because the colored race chooses to put that construction upon it. (551)

Justice John Marshall Harlan, in an enduring dissent later used to support the rejection of the separate but equal doctrine, argued that the Constitution made laws such as the Louisiana law unenforceable. Harlan believed that the Thirteenth Amendment should be read broadly to prohibit "the withholding or the deprivation of any right necessarily inhering in freedom." In short, for Harlan, the Amendment, "decreed universal civil freedom in this country." Harlan connected the Thirteenth Amendment to the Fourteenth, arguing that the inadequacy of the Thirteenth Amendment to secure fundamental equality of citizenship resulted in the ratification of the Fourteenth Amendment which, "added greatly to the dignity and glory of American citizenship, and to the security of personal liberty. . . ."

Harlan eloquently described the Fourteenth Amendment as one which made "notable additions to the fundamental law" which "were welcomed by friends of liberty throughout the world" (555). The Fourteenth Amendment provisions have a "common purpose, namely, to secure to a race recently emancipated, a race that through many generations have been held in slavery, all the civil rights that the superior race enjoy" (555–556). In a phrase for which Harlan has become well known, he argued that the "Constitution is colorblind, and neither knows nor tolerates classes among citizens . . . all citizens are equal before the law" (559). He went on to state, in prescient words, that the judgment rendered by the Court would, "in time, prove to be quite as pernicious as the decision made by this tribunal in the Dred Scott case"; on this point he was quite right. Equally correct was his assertion that

> If laws of like character should be enacted in the several states of the Union, the effect would be in the highest degree mischievous. Slavery as an institution tolerated by law, would, it is true, have disappeared from our country; but there would remain a power in the states, by sinister legislation, to interfere with the full enjoyment of the blessings of freedom, to regulate civil rights, common to all citizens, upon the basis of race, and to place in a condition of legal inferiority a large body of American citizens. . . . (563)

The character and extent of the public wrongs wrought by Jim Crow laws are difficult to convey to readers who are today accustomed to a society free from state-sanctioned segregation.[4] Consider the following examples of Jim Crow laws as descriptive of the mentality endorsed by the *Plessy* Court and confronted by Marshall and Warren at the time of the *Brown* arguments. Florida and North Carolina both had laws specifying that textbooks used by black and white children be stored separately and that precautions be taken to ensure that they were not commingled. Mississippi outlawed the printing or distribution of materials advocating social equality of or interracial marriage between whites and blacks. Six states prohibited the chaining together of Negro and white chain-gang prisoners.[5] Despite this patchwork of ignoble laws, Virginia attorney general, Lindsey J. Almond Jr., argued in defense of the Virginia system of segregation, apparently with a straight face, that Marshall was asking the Court to disturb the unfolding evolutionary process of education where from the darkest days of the depraved institution of slavery, with the help and the sympathy and the love and respect of the white people of the South, the colored man has risen under that educational process to a place of eminence and respect throughout this nation. [That system] has served him well. . . . (Kluger, 673)

Chief Justice Warren argued in the first *Brown* opinion that the *Plessy* rationale of separate but equal facilities or treatment is inapplicable to public education because it violates the Fourteenth Amendment guarantee of equal treatment under the law for all citizens. Warren began the substantive section of his opinion by tracing the history of the Fourteenth Amendment and the *Plessy* separate but equal doctrine.[6]

Warren then set out the new and compelling question presented by *Brown*: Where racially segregated schools were equal in measurable ways, was some tangible benefit given to white children, but denied to black children? (347 U.S. 483, 492, 493). In short, Warren set out the task of the Court as looking "to the effect of segregation itself on public education" (492). Lower courts had already determined that equalizing had, in fact, been undertaken and varying levels of success had been achieved in areas ranging from buildings to teacher salaries. Warren presented the question against the landscape of the educational cases which preceded *Brown*, but which did not address equalized circumstances. Instead, these cases simply compared educational facilities and found them unequal and, therefore, unconstitutional.

Warren argued that education is a fundamental duty of the state and concluded that "in the field of public education the doctrine of separate but equal has no place." "Separate educational facilities," he continued, "are inherently unequal" (495). Warren's rationale was that such treatment was particularly harmful to grade and high school students who when separated from others of similar age and qualifications would feel inferior in terms of community status, "affect[ing] their hearts and minds in a way unlikely to ever be undone" (494). Indeed, Warren cited no fewer than five non-judicial sources to support his finding that segregation had a deleterious effect on children. Warren concluded the first *Brown* opinion with a series of questions upon which all parties, and the United States

Attorney General were required to present further argument during the ensuing Court term.

Warren avoided a Court decree specifying the method of desegregation required by the Court. Warren justified his decision not to move further than finding segregated education unconstitutional by noting that the case presented a complicated set of class actions invoking the practice and law of several states and localities. He asked, in that context, for the "full assistance of the parties in formulating decrees" (495) appropriate to each locale and restored the case to the docket. In addition to the complexity of the case, Warren likely wanted to introduce integrated education slowly.

While the first *Brown* opinion offered a forthright and ethically grounded repudiation of educational segregation, the second *Brown* opinion, in language even briefer than the initial opinion, offered little in the way of certainty or support for the actual effort of desegregation. The opinion essentially returned the matter to the states, requiring lower courts, principally at the state level, and if necessary at the federal level, to oversee state efforts to revise the rules and practice of educational funding and delivery. While the NAACP argued for immediate desegregation of all public schools, the Court failed to deliver on the promise implied in the first *Brown* decision, by choosing not to impose its own standard of educational practice. Indeed, Warren adopted an "equitable" approach to resolving "varied local school problems." Warren wrote

> School authorities have the primary responsibility for elucidating, assessing and solving these problems; courts will have to consider whether the action of school authorities constitutes good faith implementation of the governing constitutional principles. Because of their proximity to local conditions and the possible need for further hearings, the courts which originally heard these cases can best perform this judicial appraisal. (349 U.S. 294, 299)

The consequence of this decision was to return the cases to the very courts which had consistently approved segregation plans. It also placed the real burden of creating desegregation plans on the poorly financed and understaffed plaintiffs and the NAACP. Warren was cognizant of the obvious difficulty this course of action presented to both. He believed however that the authority of the Supreme Court would serve as sufficient deterrent to any malicious judicial or legislative action. Warren placed the burden of demonstrating the need for any delay in desegregating the schools on the defendants, charging them with the responsibility of devising concrete plans to immediately effectuate the will of the court. In words which will be remembered always, sometimes disparagingly, Warren concluded the second *Brown* opinion by ordering the defendants to "admit to public schools on a racially nondiscriminatory basis *with all deliberate speed* the parties to these cases" (301; emphasis added). It is precisely because the states refused to integrate schools at any pace that some believe Warren abdicated his responsibility.

Dennis Hutchinson suggests that the Court privately hoped that then President Eisenhower would instruct the Department of Justice to support the efforts of the plaintiffs (Hall et al., 94). However, Eisenhower promised only to "obey the law of the land." Southern legislators were vociferous in their opposition to implementing any sort of plan to desegregate schools. The Court, in the face of this defiance, declined to hear further cases addressing issues of racial segregation until the 1958 *Cooper v. Aaron* (358 U.S. 1 1958) case, which did not produce an opinion of the magnitude or import of *Brown*. The Court did issue a series of opinionless orders, consistent with the logic of *Brown*, invalidating regulations segregating parks, golf courses, and public transportation. Finally in 1968, fully thirteen years after the second *Brown* opinion, the Court issued a decision in *Green v. County School Board of New Kent County* (391 U.S. 430 1968) which held that compliance with the *Brown* decision required genuine integration as opposed to the common and disheartening practice of repealing segregation laws but maintaining segregation practices. Cass Sunstein calls *Brown* "the most celebrated Supreme Court decision of the twentieth century" (56). On that he is certainly quite right. One measure of the importance of the decision is the enduring difficulty of the questions it both answered, and left for the future.[7]

Earl Warren

"Marshall called Warren the greatest leader I've ever run across in my life. He was likable, but firm. I know one day he came into my office, my chambers, when I got on the Court, and I said, hey, what's up? And he said something. I said, Well, Chief, look not to mention that you're the chief judge and I'm just a little old justice. But I mean, I'm a little younger than you are. Why don't you just get your secretary to call me, and I'm on the way. He says, I don't operate that way. " (Rowan, 218)

Earl Warren served as Chief Justice during a profoundly turbulent period in U.S. legal and social history. He presided over the Court as it addressed cases covering a wide variety of significant questions about individual rights. The Warren Court not only decided these highly controversial cases, but changed the way the Supreme Court thought about law.[8] In addition to the *Brown* decision, the Warren Court decided a series of landmark personal freedoms and protections cases. *Baker v. Carr* (396 U.S. 186 1962), a case Warren called the most vital decision of his tenure on the Court, adopted the one person, one vote principle. *Gideon v. Wainwright* (372 U.S. 335 1963) extended the right to legal representation in criminal proceedings to the states. *Griswold v. Connecticut* (381 U.S. 479 1965) defined further the individual right to privacy. *Miranda v. Arizona* (384 U.S. 436 1966), authored by Warren, impose the requirement that criminal suspects must be informed of basic legal rights when they are arrested. From this case we get the "Miranda warnings," and the odd verb, "to mirandize."

Warren was committed to social justice and the protection of the individual from state and federal intrusions on basic rights. Indeed, Warren, and most of the Court he presided over, was not hesitant to fit the Constitution around their judicial visions. *Griswold* demonstrates the willingness of the Warren Court to create Constitutional support for rights they believed must exist in any civilized society, though not explicitly enumerated in the Constitution. Despite the absence of an overtly stated right to privacy in the Constitution, the Warren Court 'found' such a right inuring in the rights specifically stated therein. While Warren has become definitional of judicial activism, he was not unopposed in this regard on his Court.

The scholarly and controversial Justice Felix Frankfurter was consistently critical of Warren both personally and professionally, believing Warren to be a politician in training and thought, rather than a justice, though Frankfurter appears to have been supportive of Warren's efforts in the *Brown* matter.

Warren was a three term governor of the State of California prior to his appointment to the bench by President Eisenhower. His prior experience also included a four year stint as California's attorney general and an unsuccessful run for vice president on the Thomas Dewey ticket in 1948. He grew up in Bakersfield, California, a place in which he says in his *Memoirs* he was exposed to "crime and vice of all kinds countenanced by a corrupt government." His early employment was menial, and appears to have left him with a sense of the life of the average person. It is not difficult to see how these themes emerged in his judicial life. Warren never claimed to be a scholarly justice. Indeed, the commencement of his judicial career was as a Supreme Court justice, hence, he had no experience in or really of the judiciary charged with the interpretation of the Constitution. Instead of technical or intellectual expertise, he relied on a fundamental orientation to fairness and a willingness to reflect on the constitutional parameters set forth for government in developing and implementing his judicial philosophy.

Warren joined the Court following its formal acceptance of the *Brown* case and after the initial argument of the case. Bernard Schwartz reports that Justice Frankfurter said to his clerks following the death of Chief Justice Vinson that Vinson's death was "the first indication that I have ever had that there is a god" (286). Despite the enthusiasm with which Frankfurter greeted the replacement of Vinson, Warren had much about which to be concerned. He joined the Court in an interim capacity, pending congressional confirmation. The Court that heard the initial arguments was divided on the case and had been led by a chief justice, Fred Vinson, who supported retaining the *Plessy* rationale. Furthermore, some of those on the Court who personally opposed segregation, harbored doubts about whether the Court had the Constitutional authority to outlaw it.

Moreover, Warren would be confronted by senators from southern states on the Judiciary Committee that would review his nomination and decide whether to confirm him, who would be aware that *Brown* was pending and likely would be hostile to a result favoring integration. Finally, Warren was thrust into a situation quite unlike any he had worked in before. He had little authority relative to his associates, even less given his tenuous status, a position not at all like governing or serving as attorney general, positions in which people worked for him not with him.[9] Warren, in short, had "only informal opportunities to exercise leadership." He made the most of these opportunities, however, cultivating what one of his biographers calls "presence" (161).

Warren was under pressure from President Eisenhower as well. While the case was pending, Eisenhower invited Warren to the White House for dinner. Warren, of course, was loathe to decline a summons from the President, his patron, and attended the dinner. Eisenhower pressed him, obliquely, on the *Brown* case. Rowan reports that Eisenhower said, among other things, that southerners were not bad people, only that they wished to ensure that "their sweet little girls [were] not required to sit in school alongside some big, overgrown Negroes." It appears as though Warren's only response to the President was the series of opinions. Rowan suggests that Warren may have used this unthinkable breach of conduct to sway other justices as they considered the case (216).

Warren developed an approach to the case which permitted all parties a measure of comfort. Realizing that the decision would have long-term and wide impact, Warren let his associate justices mull the case over extensively. He kept the case on their minds by circulating draft versions of an opinion that clearly separated the case into two levels of analysis and decision: first, whether the Fourteenth Amendment was violated by separate but equal schools and second, how the Court should remedy the situation should it decide in favor of the Plaintiffs. Presumably this tactic had two objectives: to achieve unanimity and the concomitant moral force a unified decision would communicate and, second, to give all parties involved an opportunity to begin to adjust to the notion that the Jim Crow laws were short-lived. In issuing such a series of opinions,

Warren believed that the impact of actual desegregation would be separated from the command to end it, permitting southern states some time to acclimate themselves to the order of the Court and to begin to act accordingly. In this belief, Warren betrays his odd, and perhaps naive belief, that faced with a choice, people would opt for fairness.

Warren drafted the *Brown* opinions, particularly the first, in language easily accessible to ordinary citizens and readily quoted in the print media. He believed that such an approach would move the opinion beyond the somewhat arcane confines of the Court and legislative bodies. He understood the *Brown* case to present a fundamental question of human rights, not one of sophisticated legal judgment. His election to write an opinion for those most likely to be affected by it demonstrates a courage of conviction. Warren took the issue of desegregation directly to the people in language they could respond to and challenged them to evaluate a practice, segregation, which said of one group of human beings that they were inferior. Warren apparently had little time for the argument made by both blacks and whites that separate and truly equal facilities might be better for both groups. Indeed, Warren is strangely silent in both opinions on this notion, though he must have been aware that it was not a narrowly held position. It is important to note that Warren had the opportunity to write the *Brown* opinions solely because of his appointment as chief justice. Seniority dictates authorship of opinions for all but the chief justice, and Warren seized the opportunity not only to draft the opinions himself, but to manage the informal conversations and formal deliberations among the justices regarding the case.

Many believe that the greatest achievement of Warren's tenure on the Court was "massing a Court unanimous in both vote and opinion" (Hall et al., 94) in the *Brown* case. His approach to move the Court to that point shows an ability for leadership of significant proportions. Not only did he devise a long-term method of deliberation to ease his associate justices toward the unanimous opinion, but he persuaded at least two justices to change their minds with respect to opinions they had created: Justice Reed intended to dissent and Justice Jackson intended to concur. Justice Frankfurter, who, like Justice

Jackson, could "talk, write, and think rings around the Chief Justice" (Kluger, 683) may not have been on Warren's side at the outset either. Warren's forceful rhetoric and depth of conviction appear to be responsible for these shifts. White believes that "the forging of a unanimous majority for the *Brown* decision established [Warren's] presence on the Court." "The task," White continues, "was one especially suited to his skills: It involved convincing others of the necessity for an arm of government to act decisively and affirmatively where a moral issue was at stake" (163).

Thurgood Marshall

> "I have to keep believing, because I know our cause is right. Justice and reason are on our side. Everybody knows this but those enslaved to customs that say whites are whites and Negroes are Negroes and never the twain shall meet." (Marshall quoted in Rowan, 207)

Thurgood Marshall, the great grandson of a slave, served as the first black associate justice of the Supreme Court. He studied law at Howard University Law School under Charles Hamilton Houston, the dean of the law school and a civil rights activist himself. Marshall authored a number of significant opinions during his tenure on the Court.[10]

Arguably, Marshall's greatest accomplishments came not as a justice but as an attorney practicing before the Court. Marshall is responsible for at least twenty-nine Supreme Court victories while serving as special counsel to the NAACP and later as director of the NAACP Legal Defense and Educational Fund, Inc. As an attorney, Marshall was, by all accounts, a skillful legal tactician and effective oral advocate. Marshall survived a brutal nomination process in 1961 when President John F. Kennedy selected him for a vacancy on the U.S. Court of Appeals for the Second Circuit. Four years later, President Lyndon Johnson named Marshall the first black solicitor general. In 1967, Johnson appointed Marshall to a vacancy on the Court created by the retirement of Justice Tom C. Clark.

The team Marshall led in the fight to win the *Brown* decision included his deputy, Jack Greenberg, a number of the best black lawyers in America, most of them graduates and teachers of Howard University Law School, and several equally gifted white lawyers. Some of these served on the ACLU staff, others on law school faculties. Most of them were Jews with a profound desire to see racial justice done in America. Listening to the arguments crafted by this team and delivered by Marshall

> . . . were nine very troubled white men: Chief Justice Fred M. Vinson, a sixty-two-year-old Kentuckian who had been appointed by Harry Truman; Stanley F. Reed, sixty-eight, another Kentuckian, the man who had delivered the decision in the Lyons murder case that crushed Thurgood Marshall's heart for a while; Felix Frankfurter, seventy, the only Jew on the Court and a conservative who showed resistance to "activist" decisions that changed anything unnecessarily; Robert H. Jackson, sixty, the former chief counsel for the United States at the Nuremburg trials; Harold H. Burton, sixty-four, a former mayor of Cleveland, Ohio; Tom C. Clark of Texas, fifty-three, former U.S. Attorney General; Sherman Minton, sixty-two, a former senator from Indiana who had bent toward the conservative side; Hugo Black, sixty-six, an Alabaman and former member of the Ku Klux Klan who had become a liberal and vocal defender of civil liberty; and William O. Douglas, fifty-four, who joined Black as the most conspicuous of the Court's advocates of equality for American Negroes. (Rowan, 195)

Perhaps the most compelling circumstance surrounding the *Brown* arguments was the deep ambivalence of the black community about desegregation. Profoundly hurtful and malicious as the Jim Crow laws were, blacks were deeply divided on the question of whether they could or should be educated by and with whites. Many believed, quite deeply, that separate education, if truly equal in terms of facilities and expenditures, was not only appropriate, but preserved black heritage and integrity (Greenberg, 86, 88). In so believing, they opposed Marshall in his effort to desegregate rather than equalize the public schools. Illustrative of this way of thinking was the Memphis branch of the NAACP which, in 1950, opposed the practice of allowing blacks into the public zoo on Thursdays only not by arguing for integrated access, but rather, for access proportionate to population and citizenship (86). Instead of opposing the practice of segregation, the Memphis branch asked only that it be done fairly. Jack Greenberg recalls that Marshall said about that decision, "the easy part of the job is fighting white folks" (86).

Marshall was aware of, but unswayed by this argument, believing that true equality could be found only in a system where each had access to all. Marshall worked for the adoption in 1950 by the national convention of the NAACP of a policy that the LDF would file only cases asking for the eradication of segregation, eschewing cases asking only that segregation be done in reasonable ways (Greenberg, 85). Marshall would not accommodate those, some of whom worked with him, who argued for a course of litigation that would ensure only equally adequate educational facilities, rather than desegregated ones. Instead, he propelled the *Brown* cases to the Court asking for nothing less than a finding that segregated schools violated the constitutional amendment for which, in many ways, the Civil War was fought.

Marshall struggled mightily to do this. Greenberg describes the preparation for the arguments in the *Brown* case and the environment in which they took place as such that Marshall was physically worn to the point of sickness. The pressure came not just from the intense intellectual difficulty in preparing to argue a case before the highest tribunal in the land, but from the need to legitimize for his constituency the decision to do so and in the way chosen. Marshall led through the strength of his character and with a champion's spirit, asking for "an end to desegregation" and nothing else (Greenberg, 85).

Admirable leadership is grounded in an unflagging commitment to the primacy of principle. The good leader must, perhaps above all else, hold unflagging convictions from which conduct flows. Jack Kemp, in a speech at the Shavano Institute for National Leadership seminar said that leadership in the context of the law ought to enable citizens to "achieve the ideal of the American founding: liberty constrained not by law, but by character" (*Imprimis*, n.p.). In both Earl Warren and Thurgood Marshall this sort of liberty became the law of the land. *Brown v. Board of Education* represents all that is right about the people and institutions of law. Warren and Marshall, from profoundly different perspectives, but each believing in the absolute inviolability of the principle that all people are equal, forged a new system for the education of the children of this country. At the same time, they brought to an effective end the legality of withholding any public accommodation from a person based on race. Without Warren and Marshall, *Brown* would not have occurred at the point in history that it did. As significantly, without either, the stature of the Court and the legal process itself would have suffered a blow proportionate to that delivered by the *Plessy* decision. Marshall and Warren led both the law and their respective constituents to a new level.

Notes

1. In pertinent part, "Section 1. All persons born or naturalized in the United States, and subject to the jurisdiction thereof, are citizens of the United States and of the State wherein they reside. No State shall make or enforce any law which shall abridge the privileges or immunities of citizens of the United States; nor shall any State deprive any person of life, liberty, or property without due process of law; nor deny to any person within its jurisdiction the equal protection of the laws.

    Section 5. The Congress shall have power to enforce, by appropriate legislation, the provisions of this article."

2. Harry W. Jones in an introduction to the text of the *Brown* I decision in *An American Primer*, edited by Daniel Boorstin, says "No case in Supreme Court history was ever presented more exhaustively by the advocates for both sides, or weighed more carefully by the members of the Court" (929).

3. "Section 1. Neither slavery nor involuntary servitude, except as a punishment for crime whereof the party shall have been duly convicted, shall exist within the United States, or any place subject to their jurisdiction.

    Section 2. Congress shall have power to enforce this article by appropriate legislation."

4. Cass R. Sunstein says in his book *The Partial Constitution* that the *Plessy* "set of understandings . . . has so completely collapsed that the notion that the world of segregation should be treated as part of a voluntary and law-free sphere of society seems unintelligible" (45). Sunstein does some profoundly interesting work on the legal reasoning in and long-term effects of the *Brown* decisions which is beyond the scope of this essay but which is highly recommended.

5. See Rowan, *Dream Makers, Dream Breakers: The World of Thurgood Marshall*, page 186 for further examples.

6. Several cases diminished the *Plessy* doctrine before the *Brown* Court eradicated it from public education. The two of greatest significance were *Sweatt v. Painter* and *McLaurin v. Oklahoma State Board of Regents*. A significant step was taken when the Court invalidated segregation in graduate schools in 1950 in the *McLaurin* case. McLaurin applied to and was denied admission by Oklahoma's all-white state university. A federal district court ordered his admission, and as a result of an Oklahoma law requiring separate education, he was segregated within the

university: he sat in a separate classroom row reserved "for Negroes," he studied at a separate library desk and ate at a reserved cafeteria table. Returning to the district court and then to the Supreme Court, McLaurin argued successfully that such treatment denied him his rights under the Fourteenth Amendment. In *Sweatt*, a companion case, the Court simultaneously struck a Texas law prohibiting Heman Sweatt, a mail carrier, from entering the University of Texas Law School. In *Sweatt*, Chief Justice Fred Vinson, who would later be succeeded by Earl Warren, held that a law school created by the state of Texas for blacks only violated the Fourteenth Amendment in response to argument by Thurgood Marshall, then chief legal counsel for the NAACP Justice Vinson reasoned, in language and logic which would be adopted in the *Brown* decision, that separate facilities would lack immeasurable elements which make one school more prestigious than another such as distinguished faculty and alumni prestige.

7. An exhaustive history of the Brown decision is contained in Richard Kluger's book *Simple Justice: The History of Brown v. Board of Education and Black America's Struggle for Equality*.

8. A fascinating examination of this shift in judicial methodology is presented in Richard Gaskins's book *Burdens of Proof in Modern Discourse*, in which he considers the Warren Court's reformulation of the burden of proof in racial discrimination cases. Gaskin argues that this shift in the burden of proof, as one might suspect from the *Brown* cases, makes it difficult for any public entity to discriminate on the basis of race even when they do so to remedy past acts of discrimination.

9. G. Edward White in *Earl Warren: A Public Life* describes this precarious position this way: ". . . he could not replace older, incompatible justices with new ones more aware of his executive style as he had done with personnel in California. He could not cultivate the press; judges did not hold press conferences. He had no powers of the purse, being beholden to Congress for appropriations, no ability to expand his personal staff, few perquisites of office" (161).

10. These cases include *Stanley v. Georgia*, a First Amendment case providing the private right to possess obscene materials in one's own home, *Police Department of Chicago v. Mosely*, providing that government may not favor some types of speech with greater protection than others, and *Linmark Associates, Inc. v. Township of Willingboro*, which prohibited restrictions on "for sale" signs motivated by a fear of "white flight." In addition, Marshall wrote several dissents of importance. In *Dandridge v. Williams* and *San Antonio Independent School District v. Rodriguez*, Marshall criticized the Court's methodology in assessing equal protection cases.

Works Cited

Boorstin, Daniel, ed. *An American Primer*. New York: Penguin, 1966.

Gaskins, Richard. *Burdens of Proof in Modern Discourse*. New Haven: Yale University Press, 1993.

Greenberg, Jack. *Crusader in the Courts*. New York: Basic Books, 1994.

Hall, Kermit L. et al., eds. *Oxford Companion to the Supreme Court of the United States*. New York: Oxford University Press, 1992.

Kemp, Jack. Speech at Hillsdale College. *Imprimis* (Newsletter of Hillsdale College), August 1994. No page numbers.

Kluger, Richard. *Simple Justice: The History of Brown v. Board of Education and Black America's Struggle for Equality*. New York: Knopf, 1976.

Rowan, Carl T. *Dream Makers, Dream Breakers: The World of Thurgood Marshall*. Boston: Little, Brown, 1993.

Schwartz, Bernard. *A History of the Supreme Court*. New York: Oxford University Press, 1993.

Sunstein, Cass R. *The Partial Constitution*. Cambridge: Harvard University Press, 1993.

Warren, Earl. *The Memoirs of Earl Warren*. Garden City, NY: Doubleday, 1977.

White, G. Edward. *Earl Warren: A Public Life*. New York: Oxford University Press, 1982.

8

Reflections on Gender, Work, and Leadership

Judith Lorber

Twenty-five years ago, Muriel F. Siebert bought a seat on the New York Stock Exchange, the first woman to be permitted to do so. In 1992, receiving an award for her accomplishments, she said bluntly that despite the numbers of women coming into high finance, the professions, and government, the arenas of power are still overwhelmingly dominated by men. The numbers bear her out.

In 1980 in the United States, only two women were chief executive officers of the largest corporations, the Fortune 500. They were Katherine Graham, chief executive of the Washington Post Company, and Marion O. Sandler, co-chief executive of Golden West Financial Corporation, in Oakland, California. In 1985, there were three: Graham, Sandler, and Elisabeth Claiborne of the Liz Claiborne clothing company. In 1990, there were also three: Graham, Sandler, and Linda Wachner of the Warnaco Group, Inc., New York. In 1992, Charlotte Beers became chief executive of Ogilvie & Mather Worldwide, the fifth largest international advertising agency, with billings of $5.4 billion, making her the world's highest ranking woman executive in that field. Linda Wachner (earning $3.1 million in 1991) was the first woman in *Fortune*'s "roster of exorbitantly paid executives" (Strom 1992, C1). Thus, in the past decade in the United States, where women composed between 42.4 and 45.4 percent of the work force, and numbered between 42.1 and 53.5 million, a total of five women were heads of the largest corporations (Marsh 1991). When *Fortune* culled the lists of the highest paid officers and directors of 799 U.S. industrial and service companies, out of 4,012 it found 19 women, or less than one-half of 1 percent.

The belief that upward mobility and leadership positions would automatically follow if women increased their numbers in the workplace greatly underestimated the social processes that get some people onto the fast track and systematically derail others. These processes are used by those at the top to ensure that those coming up will be as similar as possible to themselves so that their values and ideas about how things should be done will be perpetuated. The markers of homogeneity are gender, race, religion, ethnicity, education, and social background. The few heterogeneous "tokens" who make it past the gatekeepers first must prove their similarity to the elite in outlook and behavior. The numbers at the bottom in any field have little relation to the numbers at the top, where power politics is played and social policies are shaped.

The gender segregation so evident in the modern work world is exacerbated at the top echelons of business, the professions, and politics by gendered concepts of authority and leadership potential. Women are seen as legitimate leaders only in areas considered of direct concern to women, usually health, education, and welfare. Women's accomplishments in men's fields tend to be invisible or denigrated by the men in the field, and so women rarely achieve the stature to be considered leaders in science or space, for example. The U.S. National Aeronautics and Space Administration put 25 women pilots through rigorous physical and psychological testing from 1959 to 1961. Thirteen demonstrated "exceptional suitability" for space flight, but neither they nor 17 women with advanced science degrees were chosen to be astronauts or space scientists, even though the Russians had sent Valentina Tereshkova into space in 1963 (McCullough 1973). As Gloria Steinem said, recalling these invisible women almost 20 years later, women's demonstrating they have the "right stuff" turns into the "wrong stuff" without the approval of the men in charge (1992).

When a leader is chosen among colleagues, women are often overlooked by the men of the group, and there are usually too few women to support one another. Even where women are the majority of workers, men tend to be favored for positions of authority because women and men will accept men leaders as representing their general interests but will see women as representing only women's interests (Izraeli 1984). As a result, men in occupations where most of the workers are women, such as nursing and social work, tend to be overrepresented in high-level administrative positions, and women in occupations where most of the workers are men rarely reach the top ranks (Williams 1989, 95-98; Zunz 1991).

The Glass Ceiling

The pervasive phenomenon of women going just so far and no further in their occupations and professions has come to be known as the *glass ceiling*. This concept assumes that women have the motivation, ambition, and capacity for positions of power and prestige, but invisible barriers keep them from reaching the top. They can see their goal, but they bump their heads on a ceiling that is both hidden and impenetrable. The U.S. Department of Labor defines the glass ceiling as the "bias that prevent qualified individuals from advancing upward in their organization into management level positions" (L. Martin 1991, 1).

A recent study of the pipelines to power in large-scale corporations conducted by the U.S. Department of Labor found that the glass ceiling was lower than previously thought—in middle management. Members of disadvantaged groups were even less likely than white women to be promoted to top positions, and the upper rungs were "nearly impenetrable" for women of color (L. Martin 1991). A random sample of ninety-four reviews of personnel in corporate headquarters found that of 147,179 employees, 37.2 percent were women and 15.5 percent were minorities. Of these employees, 31,184 were in all levels of management, from clerical supervisor to chief executive officer; 16.9 percent were women and 6 percent were minorities. Of 4,491 managers at the level of assistant vice president and higher, 6.6 percent were women and 2.6 percent were minorities. Thus, in this survey, the higher the corporate position, the smaller the proportion of women; if the numbers of women in the top ranks had been proportional with the number of women in the lower ranks, over a third of the vice presidents, presidents, and executive officers would have been women. There was no separate breakdown of these figures for women of color, but another report cited by the Labor Department indicated that they make up 3.3 percent of the women corporate officers, who make up only 1 to 2 percent of all corporate officers.

As of 1990, 43.5 percent of public-sector employees in lower-level jobs were women, but they were only 31.3 percent of the department heads, division chiefs, deputies, and examiners in state and local government agencies (Strom 1992). African American women were 9.8 percent of the workers at lower levels, 5.1 percent at the top levels.

The ways that most people move up in their careers are through *networking* (finding out about job opportunities through word-of-mouth and being recommended by someone already there), *mentoring* (being coached through the informal norms of the workplace), and *sponsorship* (being helped to advance by a senior colleague). In civil service bureaucracies, where promotion depends on passing a test or getting an additional credential, those who receive encouragement and advice from senior members of the organization tend to take the qualifying tests or obtain the requisite training. In the sciences, research productivity depends to a significant degree on where you work, whom you work with, and what resources are available to you. All these processes of advancement depend on the support of colleagues and superiors, which means that in a workplace where men outnumber women and whites outnumber any other racial ethnic group, white women and women and men of disadvantaged racial ethnic groups have to be helped by white men if they are to be helped at all.

An in-depth study of nine Fortune 500 companies with a broad range of products and services located in different parts of the country found that despite differences in organizational structure, corporate culture, and personnel policies, the same practices result in a glass ceiling for women, especially women of color (L. Martin 1991). These practices were recruitment policies for upper-management levels that depended on word-of-mouth networking and employee referrals. When "head hunters" were used, they were not instructed to look for women and men of social groups underrepresented at managerial levels. The few white women and women and men of color who were already hired were not given the opportunity to build up their credentials or enhance their careers by assignment to corporate committees, task forces, and special projects. These are traditional avenues of advancement, since they bring junior members into contact with senior members of the organization and give them visibility and the chance to show what they can do. There was no monitoring of evaluation or compensation systems that determine salaries, bonuses, incentives, or perks to make sure that white women and women and men of color were getting their fair share. In general, "monitoring for equal access and opportunity, especially as managers move up the corporate ladder to senior management levels where important decisions are made, was almost never considered a corporate responsibility or part of the planning for developmental programs and policies" (L. Martin 1991, 4). In short, none of the white men in senior management saw it as their responsibility to sponsor white women or women and men of color to be their replacements when they retired.

Men in traditional women's occupations report the opposite phenomenon. Their minority status turns out to be a career advantage. Christine Williams's study of 76 men and 23 women in nursing, teaching, librarianship, and social work in the United States, whom she interviewed from 1985 to 1991, found that the men were tracked into the more prestigious, better-paying specialties within the occupation, and urged by their mentors, mostly other men, to move into positions of authority. Most of these men were white, so they were the most advantaged workers. For them not to move up to supervisory and administrative positions was considered inappropriate. As a result, they were on a "glass escalator," Williams says: "Often, despite their intentions, they face invisible pressures to move up in their professions. As if on a moving escalator, they must work to stay in place" (1992, 256). But they sometimes faced a glass ceiling at higher levels. The affirmative action policies of many institutions make the women deans and heads of departments in the women's areas too visible for them to be replaced by men (257).

Although these processes may seem benign, the imbalance of lower-level workers with disadvantaged social characteristics compared to upper-level workers with advantaged social characteristics implies a deliberate, though unstated, policy of hostility and resistance that deepens with each additional mark of disadvantage. Kimberlé Crenshaw presents a graphic analysis of who can make it through the glass ceiling.

> Imagine a basement which contains all people who are disadvantaged on the basis of race, sex, class, sexual preference, age and/or physical ability. These people are stacked—feet standing on shoulders—with those on the bottom being disadvantaged by the full array of factors, up to the very top, where the heads of all those disadvantaged by a single factor brush up against the ceiling. . . . A hatch is developed through which those placed immediately below can crawl. Yet this hatch is generally available only to those who—due to the singularity of their burden and their otherwise privileged position relative to those below—are in the position to crawl through. Those who are multiply-burdened are generally left below. (1991, 65)

Bands of Brothers

Parallel to the formal organization of a large, modern workplace, which is structured as a task-related, bureaucratic hierarchy, is the informal organization, which is based on trust, loyalty, and reciprocal favors (Lorber [1979] 1989a). Because the unspoken rules are often as significant to the way business is conducted as the written rules, colleagues want to work with people who know what goes without saying: "In order that men [*sic*] may communicate freely and confidentially, they must be able to take a good deal of each other's sentiments for granted. They must feel easy about their silences as well as about their utterances. These factors conspire to make colleagues, with a large body of unspoken understandings, uncomfortable in the presence of what they consider odd kinds of fellows" (Hughes 1971, 146).

Personal discretion and reliability are particularly necessary for those in positions of authority because of the uncertainties they face (Kanter 1977). According to Dianne Feinstein, former mayor of San Francisco who was elected to the U.S. Senate in 1992, women have to bend over backward to prove not only their competence but their trustworthiness:

> Women have to prove themselves effective and credible time and time again. Experience has taught me that the keys to a woman's effectiveness in public office are to be "trustable": to give directions clearly and to follow up, to verify every statement for accuracy, to guard her integrity carefully, and to observe the public's trust one hundred percent. Most important, she must be a team player and build relationships with her colleagues that are based on integrity and respect. (Cantor and Bernay 1992, xv)

Almost twenty years ago, Margaret Hennig and Anne Jardim predicted that conscientious and hard-working women would find it difficult to get out of middle management because their performance was geared to formal training and bureaucratic responsibilities. They felt that if women knew that senior management relies on informal networking, gathering extensive sources of knowledge from areas other than one's own, planning, policy-making, and delegating responsibility to reliable subordinates, they would be able to move up corporate career ladders (1976). Career mobility, however, does not depend only on competent performance and other efforts by the ambitious individual. To move up, a young person's worth has to be recognized and encouraged by those in the upper echelons. Promising young men of the right social characteristics are groomed for senior management by "godfathers" or "rabbis"—sponsors who take them under their wing and see to it that they learn the informal organizational rules for getting ahead. Promising young women are left to fend for themselves (Lorber 1981).

Brotherly trust among men who are business associates goes back to the nineteenth century. Before the creation of the impersonal corporation, each partner in an enterprise was personally responsible for raising capital and making a profit. Credit depended on personal trustworthiness; bankruptcy was a personal tragedy (Davidoff and Hall 1987; Silver 1990). In these transactions, the active players were all men. Women were passive partners; their money was used by kinsmen and men friends who acted as trustees. In order to cement the brotherly bonds among men who were in business together, women were encouraged to marry cousins or their brothers' partners; two sisters often married two brothers, or a brother and sister married a sister and brother; "Free choice marriage controlled in this way provided a form of security in binding together members of the middle class in local, regional and national networks, a guarantee of congenial views as well as trustworthiness in economic and financial affairs" (Davidoff and Hall 1987, 221).

In twentieth-century businesses, professions, and politics, trust and loyalty are built not through kin ties (which is considered nepotism) but through *homosociality*—the bonding of men of the same race, religion, and social-class background (Lipman-Blumen 1976). These men have the economic, political, professional, and social resources to do each other favors. Women with the same social characteristics may be included in men's circles when they have equivalent wealth, power, and social position. Most men and women, however, relate to each other socially only in familial or sexual roles (Moore 1990).

Homosociality starts early. In childhood play, boys separate themselves from girls and become contemptuous of girls' activities in their efforts to keep themselves apart. This segregation, attributed to boys' needs to establish their masculinity, makes friendship between girls and boys difficult because it is discouraged by same-gender peers. Gender grouping is not perfect in mixed-gender schools but is broached by social class and racial ethnic cross-currents and sometimes by the organizing activities of teachers. In adulthood, whenever men and women come together as equals, in coed schools and workplaces that are not gender-segregated, cross-gender friendships are undermined by intimations of sexual attraction (O'Meara 1989). One study of white middle-class young adults found that the women preferred same-gender friendships more than the men did because the men were more interested in them sexually than as companions (Rose 1985). The men invested more time and attention in their friendships with men than they did in their friendships with women, while the women gave as much emotional support to their men friends as they did to their women friends. Letty Cottin Pogrebin (1987) feels that the main reason that women and men are rarely intimate friends is that they are rarely true equals.

Although men or women may be "odd fellows" in their workplace or job, the pressures of being a woman in a man's job and a man in a woman's job are quite different. Men nurses can talk cars and sports with men physicians. In doing so, they affiliate with a higher status group, affirm their masculinity, and gain a benefit from these informal contacts in more favorable evaluations of their work. Men physicians' status is too high to be compromised by chatting with men nurses (or flirting with women nurses). Men who are openly homosexual, however, may face discrimination from men supervisors (Williams 1992, 259). Women physicians socialize with women medical students, interns, and residents, but not with women nurses. Women physicians' status is more tenuous, and they end up in a bind. They need to get along with the women nurses so that their work proceeds efficiently, yet they lose status if they bond with a lower-status group as women. Women physicians need to build colleague relationships with the men physicians who are their peers, but these men may not treat them as equals. They also need to seek sponsors among senior men who can help them advance their careers, but these men may not want them as protégées.

Because men know the power of homosocial bonding, they are discomfited when women do the same thing and often accuse such women of lesbianism, particularly because women's attentions are turned to each other and not to them. As Carol Barkalow said of the military:

> They often appear to possess an irrational fear of women's groups, believing that, in their midst, men will be plotted against, or perhaps worst of all, rendered somehow unnecessary. If women soldiers do try to develop a professional support network among themselves, they are faced with the dilemma that something as simple as two women officers having lunch together more than once might spark rumors of lesbianism—a potentially lethal charge, since even rumored homosexuality can damage an officer's career. (1990, 167–168)

Women officers who want to bond without innuendoes of homosexuality often turn to sports, which is as legitimate a place to build trust and loyalty among women as it is among men.

For the most part, as colleagues, friends, and wives, women are relegated to acting as audience or sex objects for men. According to Kathryn Ann Farr (1988), who studied a group of upper-class white men whose bonding preserved their race and class as well as their gender privileges, wives and girlfriends were needed to serve as foils for the men's exclusive sociability. The women listened as the men talked about their exploits. When the men went off on an escapade, their women warned them against getting into too much trouble, prepared food for them, and stayed behind. The men defined the boundaries of their homosocial world by excluding women, just as they maintained its racial and class exclusivity by keeping out the "wrong" kind of men. The irony is that they built their superior status in a direct and immediate way by denying their own wives and girlfriends the privileges of their race and class. In this way, the domination of men over women in their own social group is sustained, and the women collude in the process:

> These men do not view themselves as sexist, and they do not appear to be viewed by the women *with whom they interact* as sexist. In their choice of wives and girlfriends, the majority of these men seem to value independent and intelligent women. Yet their socialization into a male-dominated environment and a culture in which male sociability is highly valued causes them to think and act in ways that conflict with their intellectual assessments of the worth of and the value of social relationships with women. (Farr 1988, 269)

By excluding women who share their social characteristics from their social space, these men never have to treat women as equals or as serious competitors for positions of power.

Gender and Authority

Are men so much more acceptable in positions of authority because women "do power" differently? There tend to be two models of women's leadership styles: women are exactly like men, and women are different, but equally competent. How women or men act does not give the whole picture; women's and men's leadership styles are socially constructed in interaction and heavily influenced by the situational context and how others perceive them. If women in positions of authority tend to be more accessible, to grant more autonomy, but also to be more demanding of subordinates to perform well, the reason may be that they are in weaker positions in the organization and have fewer resources. They need subordinates' help but may be unable to reward them with raises or other perks. As a result, they ask more of subordinates but are also more likely to give concessions to those who are loyal to them, which may be perceived as contradictory behavior.

Authority in a woman is granted in a women-dominated situation, such as nursing, but questioned where authority is defined as a masculine trait, such as in police work or the military. In 1986, 10.4 percent of all uniformed U.S. Army personnel were women, but they have been underrepresented in the higher ranks. In 1988, there were nine women who were one-star generals in the U.S. military, 1.2 percent of the total, and none of higher rank. Women constituted 2 percent of the colonels, 3.5 percent of the lieutenant colonels, and 7.1 percent of other officer ranks (Barkalow 1990, 280-281). In 1991, a woman, Midshipman Juliane Gallina, was chosen the U.S. Naval Academy's brigade commander, student leader of 4,300 midshipmen. Ironically, her appointment came six months after a survey found that a "considerable segment" of students, faculty, and staff believed women had no place in the Naval Academy (Cowan 1991).

A woman leader is expected to be empathic, considerate of other's feelings, and attuned to the personal (Lorber 1985). If she is not, she is likely to be called "abrasive." As the editor of the prestigious *Harvard Business Review*, Rosabeth Moss Kanter has been publicly faulted for her confrontational management style by her associates, even though her predecessor, a man, had similar problems in his first year (Cowan 1991). Her high status as a Harvard Business School professor, corporate consultant, and author of internationally known books on management did not protect her from open criticism by her colleagues.

On the other hand, a more conciliatory style may be criticized by men and women colleagues as insufficiently authoritative. Despite the increase in women managers in the past twenty years, men and women at all career stages, including undergraduate and graduate business students, stereotype the good manager as "masculine" (Powell 1988, 145-150). Nonetheless, there are situations where a nonconfrontational approach is highly appropriate. In medicine and police work, quintessential masculine professions in American society, being able to listen and take the role of the other person may be more productive than a distancing, authoritative stance in eliciting information or deflecting conflict (S. E. Martin 1980). Conciliation and using the other person's views can be threatening to men in police work who have learned to rely on physical force and to men doctors for whom medical expertise is the ultimate authority.

If the goal for women in men-dominated situations is to be treated as if they were men, they are in a double bind, and so are the men. If the women act like men, they challenge men's "natural" right to positions of power. If the women act like women, they don't belong in a situation where they have to take charge (that is, act like a man). As Susan Ehrlich Martin says of policewomen on patrol: "The more a female partner acts like a police officer, the less she behaves like a woman. On the other hand, the more she behaves like a woman, the less protection she provides, the less adequate she is as a partner—although such behavior preserves the man's sense of masculinity. The way out of the bind is simple: keep women out of patrol work" (1980, 93–94).

Where Are We Going?

The enormous weight of history and current institutionalized practices makes it seem as if there is no way out—no way to make significant and lasting changes in the social institution of gender. Yet changes are made every day (another paradox of gender). There is constant tension between individual and group resistance and social control, between the exceptions and the rules. Indeed, the rules of existing institutions are constantly being revised and repaired (Hilbert 1987). Human beings are both orderly and rebellious; they like knowing what to expect from others, even if they protest and challenge.

Feminists have resisted and rebelled as scholars, researchers, and activists (Chafetz and Dworkin 1986). The "known world" looks very different through women's eyes. As activists, feminists have promulgated reforms of existing institutional laws, rules, and norms. As researchers, feminists have made evident the built-in oppression of women in patterns of behavior that are taken for granted, particularly concerning sexuality and violence. As theorists, feminists have turned inside out the categories of production and social reproduction by demonstrating that housework and child care are unpaid *work* for the family and for society, and that paid work is so deeply gendered that there seem to be built-in sexual taboos about how women can earn money. Lesbian feminists and gay men particularly, through their open rebellions, have changed ideas of normalcy and deviance in sexual mores, living arrangements, and parenting.

But I do not think it is inevitable that gender categories will gradually blur under the weight of evidence of the similarities of women and men, or that by gradual erosion, gender will stop being the major determinant of how the work of modern society is allocated and the rewards distributed. Pendulum swings are common and social exigencies often excuse greater oppression of one group by another. It can certainly happen to women and men.

In the United States during World War II, women were recruited for work in defense plants, steel mills, and other heavy industry. Day-care centers were set up in many workplaces because of the desperate need for workers. But despite women's evident ability to handle heavy physical labor and their desire to keep working and earning high wages, gender segregation of jobs persisted, and women were fired when the war ended. The day-care centers were abandoned, and the 1950s were conservative, family-oriented, and gender-segregated. With the crumbling of communism and the turn to capitalist economies in Eastern Europe, women workers expect to be fired first, and liberal abortion laws are under challenge from resurgent Catholic hierarchies.

Change can go the other way, too. The Persian Gulf War of 1990–1991 sent 35,000 U.S. servicewomen to the frontlines, including mothers of small children, some of whom volunteered. They were 6 percent of the total force of 541,425, and 10 percent of those who were killed. Although the disruption of family life may lead to promulgation of protective rules once again, U.S. servicewomen attained widespread public recognition of their role. ("Our men and women in the Armed Services" was the slogan of the day.) Indeed, a few months after the end of the war, the U.S. House of Representatives voted to allow women to be combat pilots.

The paradox of women fighting and dying to protect and liberate countries that don't allow their women to vote, drive cars, or appear in public unveiled seems to have raised the consciousness of women in both cultures. American servicewomen had to wear long sleeves off their bases, be accompanied into town by a man and have him pay, and use the back doors of gymnasiums and other facilities. Under orders from generals and politicians, they conformed, but grudgingly; they would have liked servicemen to give up their prerogatives in sympathy.

Because consciousness of oppression does not always lead to a push for action and rebels are frequently publicly punished, individuals are more likely to conform than to rebel. Not surprisingly, those advantaged by the social institution of gender want to maintain the status quo, but the not-so-privileged also have an investment in a going social order that gives them some bargaining power. Rebellion is hard on individual lives—it can eat up a person's livelihood, emotions, and freedom. Unless rebellion is a major group effort, supported by a substantial number of women and men, it is not likely to make a dent in an existing major institution like gender.

Real change would mean a conscious reordering of the organizing principles of social life (women take care of children, men go to work) with awareness of hidden assumptions (children have different attachments to mothers than to fathers) and latent effects (men need to suppress the feminine in themselves and can't allow women to have any authority over them). Change is unlikely to be deep-seated unless the pervasiveness of the social institution of gender and its social construction are made explicit.

Works Cited

Barkalow, Carol, with Andrea Raab. *In the Men's House*. New York: Poseidon, 1990.

Cantor, Dorothy W., and Toni Bernay. *Women in Power: The Secrets of Leadership*. Boston: Houghton Mifflin, 1992.

Chafetz, Janet Saltzman, and Anthony Gary Dworkin. *Female Revolt: Women's Movements in World and Historical Perspective*. Totowa, NJ: Rowman & Allenheld, 1986.

Cowan, Alison Leigh. "Management Citadel Rocked by Unruliness." *New York Times*. Business Section. September 26, 1991.

Davidoff, Lenore, and Catherine Hall. *Family Fortunes: Men and Women of the English Middle Class, 1780–1850*. Chicago: University of Chicago Press, 1987.

Farr, Kathryn Ann. "Dominance Bonding Through the Good Old Boys Sociability Group." *Sex Roles* 18 (1988): 259–277.

Hennig, Margaret, and Anne Jardim. *The Managerial Woman*. New York: Pocket Books, 1976.

Hilbert, Richard A. "Bureaucracy as Belief, Rationalization as Repair: Max Weber in a Post-functionalist Age." *Sociology Theory* 5 (1987): 70–86.

Hughes, Everett C. *The Sociological Eye*. Chicago: Aldine-Atherton, 1971.

Izraeli, Dafina N. "The Zionist Women's Movement in Palestine, 1911–1927: A Sociological Analysis." *Signs* 7 (1984): 87–114.

Kanter, Rosabeth Moss. *Men and Women of the Corporation*. New York: Basic Books, 1977.

Lipman-Blumen, Jean. "Toward a Homosocial Theory of Sex Roles." *Signs* 1 (1976): 15–31.

Lorber, Judith. "Trust, Loyalty, and the Place of Women in the Informal Organization of Work." In *Women: A Feminist Perspective*, 4e. ed. Jo Freeman. Mountainview, CA: Mayfield, 1989.

———. "The Limits of Sponsorship for Women Physicians." *Journal of the American Medical Women's Association* 36 (1981): 329–338.

———. "More Women Physicians: Will It Mean More Humane Health Care?" *Social Policy* 16 (1985): 50-54.

Marsh, Barbara. "Women in the Work Force." *Wall Street Journal.* October 18, 1991. B3.

Martin, Lynn. *A Report on the Glass Ceiling Initiative.* Washington D.C.: U.S. Department of Labor, 1991.

Martin, Susan Ehrlich. *Breaking and Entering: Police Women on Patrol.* Berkeley: University of California Press, 1980.

Moore, Gwen. "Structural Determinants of Men's and Women's Personal Networks." *American Sociological Review* 55 (1990): 726-735.

O'Meara, J. Donald. "Cross-Sex Friendship." *Sex Roles* 21 (1989): 525-543.

Pogrebin, Letty Cottin. *Among Friends: Who We Like, Why We Like Them and What We Do With Them.* New York: McGraw Hill, 1987.

Powell, Gary N. *Women and Men in Management.* Newbury Park, CA: Sage, 1988.

Rose, Suzanna M. "Same- and Cross-Sex Friendships and the Psychology of Homosociality." *Sex Roles* 12 (1985): 63-74.

Silver, Allan. "Friendship in Commercial Society: Eighteenth Century Social Theory and Modern Sociology." *American Journal of Sociology* 95 (1990): 1474-1504.

Strom, Stephanie. "Fashion Avenue's $100 Million Woman." *New York Times.* Business Section. May 17, 1992.

Williams, Christine L. *Gender Differences at Work: Women and Men in Nontraditional Occupations.* Berkeley: University of California Press, 1989.

———. "The Glass Escalator: Hidden Advantages for Men in the 'Female' Professions." *Social Problems* 39 (1992): 253-267.

Zunz, Sharyn. "Gender-related Issues in the Career Development of Social Work Managers." *Affilia* 6 (1991): 39-52.

9

Mujaheddin and Militiamen: The Global Challenge of Esoteric Leadership

Garth Katner

According to the now classic typology developed by James MacGregor Burns, *esoteric leadership* is a specific example of *transforming leadership*. In other words, it is a social relationship that exists at two interrelated levels. On the first, esoteric leaders pragmatically exchange scarce goods and services for the support of potential followers. On the second, higher level, leaders and their followers are more intimately related by their mutual need to fulfill less concrete, but equally important, psychological and spiritual aspirations. Yet the kinds of esoteric leadership we see emerging around the world today defy Burns's optimistic outlook. He sees transforming leaders as heroes, elevating the moral nature of their followers, helping them look forward toward more just futures.

Esoteric leaders we can observe today turn this model on its head; profoundly pessimistic of the present, the new esoteric vision tends to enshrine a belief in a less complex, more virtuous *golden age* of the past that must be restored in the immediate future.

The intense desire for simplistic answers to complex problems, underlying much of this vision, promotes an equally intense fascination with conspiracy theories of all kinds. Followers tend to support esoteric leaders who can successfully weave a complicated web of explanations from a single causal thread. The conspiracy theories that are popular among esoteric leaders and their followers share one common element: an almost rabid and therefore fundamental belief that national government is exclusively responsible for all that is wrong with their respective society, if not the world.

Esoteric leadership today is embued with a local orientation in terms of both ideology and organization. Leaders and followers are not inspired by universal ideologies which advocate fundamental global change. Esoteric leaders and their followers find ideological inspiration in a decidedly local source: the small community bound together by the traditional ties of family, ethnicity, and religion. They subsequently adopt ideologies which do not seek to change the world but to preserve and defend their communities from it.

Given the overall concern for preservation and defense, it is not surprising that esoteric leadership frequently embraces those ideologies which are colored by an aberrant paranoia of outsiders. The most obvious consequence, bigotry of an ethnic, religious, or xenophobic nature, directly affects esoteric organizations in two significant ways. First, they tend to be small, never numbering more than 50 members in a single location, because of the tendency to splinter over disagreements concerning leadership, vision, and strategies. Second, once separated, they rarely combine into larger, more centralized associations. This does not mean that esoteric organizations with similar visions and strategies do not have any contact with one another. They often do form loose networks through which leaders and followers can share information as well as other resources and services on a limited scale. Nevertheless, the orientation of each of these organizations remains local, its membership isolated, and its scope of activities narrow.

The most significant feature distinguishing esoteric leadership from other forms of transforming leadership is its active embrace of extreme violence. The esoteric vision encourages leaders and followers to perceive themselves as embattled minorities struggling against the much larger forces of evil in the world. Compromise of any kind is synonymous with utter defeat.

In many examples of esoteric leadership, this brutal pessimism underlies the glorification of violence as an end in itself. They are obsessed with war for its own sake and pursue victory at all costs. Peace to them is a lull between battles, and they glory in the use of arms. As a result, a number of militias have been amassing considerable stockpiles of weapons and supplies.

Even with all its extremism, the contemporary esoteric leadership vision is *populist* in nature. Leaders and followers believe they represent the interests of a society in which the vast majority of its members are either too ignorant or too afraid to act on their own. They appeal to this majority through a critical rhetoric that clearly articulates the nebulous concerns and frustrations of society, and also starkly highlights a single principal cause of these feelings. Rhetoric of this kind can be vicious since it tends to scapegoat specific individuals, groups, or institutions. Contemporary esoteric leadership appeals in part because of its commitment to action. Broad segments of mainstream society may not support the use of violence, but they do respect the willingness to confront complicated problems and issues. This is particularly true in societies where much of the mainstream sincerely feels powerless to affect meaningful change. The resulting humiliation and hopelessness is exploited by esoteric leaders to convince individuals that they have no alternative but to support radical measures.

The Afghan Taliban

Since 1989, when the last units of the Soviet army withdrew, Afghanistan has been divided into a series of semi-independent provinces by as many as ten *mujaheddin*, or holy warrior, militias. Over the last three years, the commanders of these militias have fought one another to dominate the central government, plunging this south-central Asian country into a devastating civil war. In 1994 alone, 34,000 Afghans were killed or wounded. Another one million Afghans remain homeless,[1] having sought refuge in neighboring countries during the ten-year war to liberate Afghanistan from the Soviet Union. The civil war has also disrupted the economy. Millions of Soviet land mines and damaged irrigation systems prevent farmers from raising even enough food for their families. Many have turned to the lucrative cultivation of opium. Outside the Afghan capital of Kabul, the central government has little real authority. The terror imposed by hundreds of criminal gangs and feuding mujaheddin has effectively undermined the rule of law. Banditry, often ending in rape or murder, is commonplace.

The first and, according to Western observers, most successful attempt to end the civil war began sometime in the summer of 1994 when Muhammed Omar, a forty-year old *mullah*, or Muslim cleric, claimed to have received a vision of the prophet Muhammed commanding him to save Afghanistan from the mujaheddin militias. By September, Omar had organized approximately 500 students from the *madrassas*, or Islamic religious schools, at his refugee camp in Pakistan. This new militia, which would quickly become known as the *Taliban* (the Urdu-Persian term for students), grew rapidly, crossed into Afghanistan and within six months took control of more than 40 percent of the country. The territory, stretching some 500 miles from the southern province of Helmand northeast to within nine miles of Kabul, was the largest ever dominated by a single militia since the beginning of the civil war (John Burns, 3).

The astonishingly rapid success of the Taliban was based, in part, on the ability of its esoteric vision to incorporate the cultural and religious elements of Afghan society. Omar blamed unscrupulous mujaheddin commanders who were no better than common criminals for the civil war. Therefore, Omar called for the complete disarmament of all militias and the subsequent creation of a government based upon Islam as well as popular support. In the interim, Afghan interests would best be represented by a neutral force of pious Muslims: not surprisingly, the Taliban themselves. In order to achieve these goals, a strict interpretation of Islamic law was imposed in the areas occupied by the Taliban. They curtailed explicit criminal activities and closely regulated the behavior of men and women in public places.

Nevertheless, the esoteric vision of the Taliban also acknowledged the incredible diversity of Afghan society where more than twenty ethnic groups practice numerous forms of Islam. The Taliban promised to tolerate a wide variety of local traditions if they did not contradict the spirit of Islamic law. At the same time, they would encourage Muslims from all of the ethnic groups to join their militia. This promise was necessary for three reasons. First, the Taliban were clearly trying to broaden their base of support both religiously and ethnically. They were predominantly Pashtoon, a southern offshoot of the Pathans who have dominated Afghanistan for centuries, and Sunni, the branch of Islam practiced by almost 90 percent of all Afghans. Second, Kabul, and hence the Afghan government, would not fall to the Taliban until the *Hezb-Allah*, or Party of God, was defeated. Not only was this the most powerful of the mujaheddin militias, but it was also the most conservative in both religious and ethnic terms (Anderson 20 February). Its leader, Gulbuddin Hekmatyar, is a fellow Pashtoon and Sunni. Consequently, the apparent tolerance of the Taliban vision was an implicit declaration of war against the Hezb-Allah.

Finally, the promise of tolerance provided the strategies of the Taliban with the necessary local orientation. Afghan society generally revolves around the family and the village. As a result, Afghans tend to be suspicious of all foreigners. This is especially true for those who have tried to impose foreign ideologies such as British imperialism and Soviet communism. Afghans are equally suspicious of those who would impose what they consider to be foreign interpretations of Islam such as the Islamic fundamentalists from Saudi Arabia, Iran, and Pakistan. They even find it difficult to trust members of other ethnic groups in Afghanistan (Singh, 8). In order to resist invasion of any kind, Afghan sons are generally trained by their fathers in the lifestyle and virtues of the warrior.

As a result, the Taliban recruited new followers and sympathizers by portraying themselves as a local-warrior militia despite their origins in Pakistan. Omar repeatedly accused the governments of Saudi Arabia, Iran, and Pakistan of interfering in Afghan affairs by giving military and financial aid to various mujaheddin militias (Smith, 5). At the same time, he rejected accusations that the Taliban were in fact organized, trained, and supplied by the Pakistani military. The Taliban further emphasized their local orientation when they chose to resolve local problems in the areas they occupied before moving forward. Their first operation in southwest Afghanistan successfully stopped mujaheddin raids on food convoys from Pakistan. Later, when they entered Kandahar, the second largest city in Afghanistan, the Taliban immediately halted the banditry, extortion, and rape committed by dozens of the feuding gangs. They burned poppy fields and jailed or executed opium traffickers. In the words of one Afghan observer: "People in those areas [that the Taliban controls] are happy with them because they don't do anything against Islam and they have helped bring peace and security" (Anderson 20 February 24).

During their six-month campaign to Kabul, the Taliban were armed with more than a convincing esoteric vision. As with the other mujaheddin militias, they were also well-armed with the weapons of war, prepared to use violence when necessary. Most of the original followers of Muhammed Omar were, like him, veterans of the war against the Soviet occupation. After their initial successes, the Taliban attracted other well-trained mujaheddin with battlefield experience, both from this war and the civil war that followed. The Taliban even included a significant number of officers and soldiers from the disbanded Afghan communist army, which had been allied with the Soviet Union. By March of 1995, when they reached Kabul, a number of observers reported that these fighters, numbering around 20,000, had built an impressive arsenal: a squadron of MiG 21 jets, 200 tanks, and several attack helicopters, as well as small arms, including U.S.-made Stinger missiles (see John Burns; Anderson 25 February).

Initially, the truly violent nature of the Taliban went unnoticed by many. For example, one international aid worker in Kandahar claimed that the Taliban would make contact with the mujaheddin of potential rival militias in order to persuade them to join the Taliban. A Western diplomat agreed, concluding, "No one wants to pull a trigger on a Talib. They are like an army of nuns" (Anderson 25 February). Nothing could be further from the truth. Quite simply, a well-stocked arsenal in the capable hands of experienced veterans permitted the Taliban the luxury of defeating a majority of their opponents without ever fighting them. Faced with an overwhelming threat of violence, the mujaheddin militias retreated, surrendered, or simply joined the Taliban.

For many Afghans who supported the Taliban in the southeastern provinces, the commitment to bold action, supported by the willingness to use violent means, was more significant than the specific goals. Aabha Dixit, an Afghan expert living in New Delhi, observed, "The most interesting thing about the Taliban is that nobody knows where they came from, where they are going. We only see them moving" (Anderson 20 February, 24). No less significant were the frustrations that Afghans felt toward the other feuding militias. As the Taliban advanced on Kabul, not only did they prove that they shared these feelings with the Afghan people, but they also showed that the end of the civil war might be in sight.

On March 19, 1995, the Taliban were brutally defeated 13 miles from Kabul by mujaheddin loyal to the President of Afghanistan, Burhanuddin Rabbani. Those who were not killed or captured retreated south to Kandahar and then into Pakistan. Little else has been reported by either the regional or international media. Obscured and ambiguous at first, the cause of this spectacular defeat has become much clearer now due primarily to hindsight. At the military level, the impressive arsenal of the Taliban was no match for the highly organized and well-trained army defending Kabul. Yet this begs an important question: Why didn't the survivors retreat, regroup, and try again? To understand the answer, one must remember Burns's principles of moral leadership discussed earlier.

Although the Taliban leadership was able to fulfill the immediate needs of its followers and sympathizers, it quickly became apparent to the latter that the price of peace and security was far too high. Taliban promises of a tolerant Islam were quickly forgotten. Individuals were summarily executed on the suspicion of dealing drugs. Unmarried lovers were publicly flogged and women were banned from shopping or working in the bazaar (Anderson 2 March). Reports of these actions preceded the Taliban as they moved out of the southern provinces. The Tajiks, who dominate the region around Kabul, were especially concerned. The provinces controlled by the Taliban are dominated by the Pashtoon. The Tajiks reasoned that if the Taliban could treat members of their own ethnic group this harshly, they would probably fare much worse as non-Pashtoons. Consequently, they chose the alternative program of remaining loyal to their own leaders who supported the Afghan president.

Similarly, the real commitments of the Taliban became increasingly apparent to Pashtoons and non-Pashtoons alike. The rumors of close ties with the Pakistani military were eventually substantiated by sources in both countries. It became an open secret that most of the original Taliban had been recruited, trained, and led by Pakistani frontier police during the first two months of their operations inside Afghanistan (Singh, 8). By the time the Taliban arrived on the outskirts of Kabul, their reputation as selfless defenders of the Afghan people had all but given way to the reality of Pashtoon freebooters in the pay of a foreign power. Clearly they had given up both their vision and responsibility for affecting meaningful change. Whatever else remained was destroyed as the Taliban bombarded Kabul in preparation for their final assault. After the battle, devastating even by Afghan standards, a Kabul resident stated: "People used to embrace them. Now we consider them just another group of warriors which has helped to destroy this city" (*Chronicle* 20 March, 10).

The U.S. Militias

In contrast to the mujaheddin militias of Afghanistan, militias in the United States first appear to vary greatly in terms of goals, strategies, and structure. Some seek to preserve the United States Constitution, others hope to make the Bible the highest law of the land. Some advocate violence as an offensive strategy, others reserve it for self-defense only. Some militias are large and well-organized, others are small, family dominated affairs. Nevertheless, they all share two important features which permit them to be classified as examples of esoteric leadership.

First, the militias share a common genealogy with previous generations of esoteric organizations. Whether or not their members are conscious of the fact, militias are related to Posse Comitatus, the survivalists, and other patriot groups (Ridgeway, 17–19). This should not be very surprising since esoteric leadership is neither new nor an isolated phenomenon in the United States. Beyond Posse Comitatus, the geneology stretches back to the Ku Klux Klan, the American Nazi Party, and the John Birch Society; these, in turn, evolved from the nativist and isolationist groups, such as the infamous Know-Nothings of the nineteenth century.

Second, the current generation of esoteric leadership shares a comprehensive vision, the elements of which remain fairly consistent among the various groups. This esoteric vision focuses primarily on the fundamental economic, cultural, and political forces responsible for transforming mainstream American life over the last two decades. According to Robert Heilbronner, scientific and technological innovations have undermined the certainties of traditional American values without successfully replacing them. Therefore, any sense of the common good has been forgotten as controversies over gender, sexuality, birth control, and abortion intensify. The certainty of prosperity, once the foundation of the American economy, is likewise threatened by increased global competition. As wages decline and unemployment increases, mainstream society struggles harder to maintain the American Dream (Heilbronner, 81; 101–102).

This situation has been exacerbated by a growing pessimism about the possibility of meaningful political change. The war in Vietnam convinced many in the American mainstream that national politicians no longer believe in American political values. Watergate persuaded others that these politicians were also willing to undermine the common good in the pursuit of their own self-centered interests. Finally, conservative leaders and pundits, including Ronald Reagan, Rush Limbaugh, and Newt Gingrich have convincingly argued that the federal government has become too powerful, too political, too cynical, and too distant from most Americans to adequately represent their interests (Wills, 50).

Every American miltia active today takes this argument one step further by asserting that the federal government is the real threat to the interests of the American people. An intense suspicion of the government, often lapsing into fear and paranoia, is the basis for this assertion. Militia publications accuse the government of undermining the civil rights defined and protected by the U.S. Constitution.[2] The steady expansion of state and federal regulations is reducing the scope of personal freedom. On the one hand, the government uses intrusive practices such as the imposition of social security numbers, the

1040 federal tax form, and the national census to limit individual autonomy. On the other hand, the very foundation of personal freedom, the right to own private property, is effectively undermined by regulations targeting business, the environment, and public safety (Davis, 16–17).

These publications also document alleged abuses by federal officials. Corrupt representatives elected from both the Democratic and Republican parties refuse to limit their prerogatives by enacting term limits or a balanced budget amendment. Law enforcement is a particular area of concern as well. Militias argue that an increasing number of violent confrontations between various groups and the federal government is evidence of a systematic attack on the rights of these groups to organize and protest against government policies. They also purport that gun control legislation such as the Brady Law is clearly designed to undermine the ability of the militias to defend themselves from brutal law enforcement officials (Campbell).

An often obsessive belief in a variety of conspiracy theories sustains each of these assertions. Either the federal government by itself has embarked upon a clandestine plan to impose a totalitarian system in America or it is merely a tool of the *shadow government*, dominated by an international network of conspirators seeking to establish a single, global government. The United Nations, multinational corporations, international bankers, the Council on Foreign Relations, and the U.S. Federal Reserve are just a few of the groups and institutions frequently accused of this international conspiracy. They allegedly exert control over the United States through any number of instruments including the Federal Emergency Management Agency, secret U.N. bases in the Midwest and Northeast housing Russian troops, and microchips, implanted in U.S. currency or individuals, used to monitor the movements of every American.

As the forwardmost line of resistance against the encroaching One World Government, as they refer to it, the militias created a network of loosely affiliated groups organized at the grass-roots level. This local orientation reflects, in part, the necessity to guarantee the survival of the militia network as a whole. The militias do not have leaders at the national level. Instead, each local militia commander is responsible for his or her own followers. Moreover many militias possess a redundant command structure consisting of most of the membership. Small, decentralized groups have a better chance for survival in the struggle against a well-organized opponent. Since no member or group is indispensable, their defeat or capture will not seriously weaken the network.

A local orientation also reflects the broader esoteric vision of the militia network. In order to avoid being regulated and monitored by the government, militia members try to remove themselves from American society as much as possible. This process, most commonly known as *living off the grid*, includes a wide range of activities. Those seeking to protest an overly intrusive government frequently refuse to pay taxes, use currency, or obtain motor vehicle licenses. More extreme are the actions of militia members who wish to isolate themselves and their families from the corrupting influence of the mainstream. Self-sufficient communities and compounds are established in rural areas in which the militias are free to educate their children, train followers, and plan their strategies against the One World Government.

Imposed isolation does have a tendency to transform a general suspicion of the government into an overall distrust of outsiders indistinguishable from most forms of bigotry. Militias from around the country have denied that their esoteric vision contains bigoted elements. However, publications with racist and anti-Semitic reputations are particularly popular with their members.[3] More revealing is the popularity of *The Turner Diaries* by William Pierce of the neo-Nazi National Alliance. This book, wildly popular among violent racist groups since the 1980s, blames many of the problems experienced by white Christians on people of color, immigrants, feminists, environmentalists, and homosexuals.

These and similar publications are also important for understanding how the militias view the use of violence as a legitimate strategy. An apocalyptic theme is interwoven in many of the conspiracy theories attributed to the militias. Its origins can be traced to the *End Times* theology of evangelical Christian churches (Barkun, 196). The fate of the United States and indeed the world depends upon a vicious struggle between the forces of good represented by the militias and the forces of evil promoting the establishment of the One World Government. The militias will eventually triumph. Nevertheless, their struggle will end only after they have utterly destroyed the evil forces in a final, horrible battle. This theme leaves the militias with three possible courses of action. First, they can adopt survivalist tactics and wait for the federal government to attack first. Second, they can become active in local politics, since many consider state and national institutions illegitimate, in the hopes of avoiding the final confrontation with the federal government by changing unacceptable policies. Third, the militias can attempt to overthrow the federal government through a bloody campaign of terror.

All militias claim to be organized purely for self-defense and the peaceful expression of political views. Except for the April 19 bombing of the federal building in Oklahoma City, in which the two alleged bombers were suspected of contacts with militias in Michigan, militias have not been directly linked to a campaign of widespread violence against the federal government or anyone else. Recent developments inside the militia network, however, point to an increasing possibility that the militias could choose the third option. The rhetoric normally used by the militias has become more aggressive and confrontational. A survey of militia-oriented postings on the Internet reveals that there was little or no sympathy for the victims of the Oklahoma City bombing. Several self-identified militia members referred to them merely as the "collateral damage of war." Others reported their optimism that the "war against the feds" was finally underway.[4]

Although it is difficult to determine just how widespread these attitudes might be, they do indicate the presence of a dangerous *warrior mentality* described earlier. As a result, a number of militias have been amassing considerable stockpiles of weapons and supplies. A series of interviews with militia members from Wisconsin and northern Michigan revealed their concerns that other militias around the country have begun to acquire the technology and materials for making bombs in the wake of the Oklahoma City bombings. The acquisition of ever-deadlier weapons is not only a response to the fears of a federal crackdown. It is also the typical act of warriors who do not wish to appear weak to either their comrades or the outside world.

More disturbing, perhaps, is the broad appeal the militias enjoy in mainstream society. Part of their success is dependent upon advanced communications technologies. Militias are now linked by the Internet, email, and fax machines. They exchange information and viewpoints through videocassettes, teleconferencing, and short-wave radio. Increasing numbers of individuals who are not militia members are listening because of the conservative rhetoric which is currently popular throughout the United States. Although most Americans certainly do not agree with their more extreme views, they do understand and support the principles of individualism, self-help, and grass-roots organization upon which the militias are supposedly based. Non-militia members can also appreciate the efforts of a group which confronts problems considered irresolvable by the rest of American society, including mainstream politicians. In short, mainstream Americans are willing to permit the militias the opportunity to fill the perceived leadership vacuum in America despite their possible moral shortcomings.

Conclusions

The militia network in the United States and the Taliban in Afghanistan raise three crucial questions for practitioners, scholars, and teachers who wish to promote the concept of moral leadership articulated by James MacGregor Burns. *First, how does esoteric leadership challenge moral leadership?* Moral leadership creates a community that is bound together by the mutuality of needs. Members treat one another as they would expect to be treated themselves. This requires open and nonviolent communication between community members as well as tolerance of those who are different.

Esoteric leadership actively undermines this type of community. The needs of some, the followers of esoteric leaders, are met at the expense of others, usually those considered outsiders. Esoteric leaders legitimize such behavior by declaring that outsiders are their enemies. These outsiders are then blamed for the perceived inability of society to provide for the needs of esoteric followers. Esoteric leaders provide their followers with scapegoats also to fulfill their psychological or spiritual needs for certainty. There can be no civil discourse within esoteric organizations or between them and the rest of society as long as esoteric leaders and their followers remain isolated and deeply fearful of outsiders. Their only alternative is violence or the threat of violence.

How then should leaders and followers who practice moral leadership respond to esoteric leaders and their followers? They must recognize that esoteric followers and those prone to following esoteric leaders have legitimate needs, physical as well as psychological and spiritual. These individuals cannot be dismissed merely as paranoids or lunatics. Instead, they must be persuaded to join a community that is based upon moral leadership. Therefore, moral leaders and their followers must confront esoteric organizations and engage them in meaningful dialogue without resorting to violence. This will be difficult because the esoteric organizations define the terms of most controversial issues in ways that limit civil discourse.

Leadership studies programs simply cannot ignore the significance of esoteric leadership, and must not pretend that leaders will follow the rules and patterns that scholars would wish them to. Students need to be prepared to understand esoteric leadership. They need to be encouraged to resist the temptations to lead with the tools of resentment and violence. And they must be educated away from the siren calls to follow leaders who teach hatred and build factions. More study of esoteric movements like the American militias and the Afghan Taliban can only broaden the purpose and the effectiveness of leadership studies.

Notes

1. This and the following data are provided by the U.S. Department of State, *Afghanistan Human Rights Practices, 1994.*

2. Publications are available through a number of sources. However, the most comprehensive can be found through "homepage" directories located on the World Wide Web. Three examples are the Patriot Information Center (http://www.parkplace.com/0/parkplace/Townsquare/patriot/patriot.html), Sovereign's WWW Content Page (http://www.primenet.com/~lion/index.html), and the Patriots WWW Page (http://www.kaiwan.com:80/~patriot).

3. These include *The Spotlight*, published by the Liberty Lobby; *New American*, published by the John Birch Society; and *Executive Intelligence Review* of Lyndon LaRouche. Chip Bartlet, "Armed Militias, Right Wing Populism, and Scapegoating," (Cambridge, MA: Political Research Associates, 1995), p. 3 available from the Information on Militias homepage (http://www.well.com/user/srhodes/militia.html).

4. <alt.conspiracy>, <talk.politics.guns>, <alt.sovereignty>, <misc.survivalism>, and <alt.activism.militia> (20, 21, and 22 April 1995).

Works Cited

Anderson, John Ward. "Student Militia Masses Outside Afghan Capital." *Washington Post*. March 2, 1995, A23-24.

———. "Afghan Militia's Rise Pushes U.N. Peace Effort Near Collapse." *Washington Post*. February 25, 1995, A1.

———. "Powerful Student Militia May Hold Key to Afghan Future." *Washington Post*. February 20, 1995, A1, 24.

Barkun, Michael. *Religion and the Racist Right: The Origins of the Christian Identity Movement*. Chapel Hill, NC: University of North Carolina Press, 1994.

Bartlet, Chip. *Armed Militias, Right Wing Populism, and Scapegoating*. Cambridge, MA: Political Research Associates, 1995.

Burns, James MacGregor. *Leadership*. New York: Harper & Row, 1978.

Burns, John F. "New Afghan Force Takes Hold, Turning to Peace." *New York Times*. February 16, 1995, A3.

Campbell, J.B. "Federal Abuses of Power Spark Militias." *The Spotlight*. January 9, 1995, 1-3.

Davis, T.L. "Under Siege." *Journal for Patriotic Justice in America*. 1 (April 1995): 16-17.

Eco, Umberto. "Ur Fascism." *New York Review of Books*. June 22, 1995, 12-15.

Heilbronner, Robert. *Visions of the Future: The Distant Past, Yesterday, Today, and Tomorrow*. New York: Oxford University Press, 1995.

Ridgeway, James. *Blood in the Face*. New York: Thunder's Mouth Press, 1990.

San Francisco Chronicle. Editorial. March 20, 1995, A10.

Schneider, Keith. "Bomb Extremists' Tactics" *New York Times*. April 26, 1995, A14.

Singh, S.K. "The Taliban Factor." *Hindustan Times*. January 5, 1995, 8-12.

Smith, Nancy DeWolf. "These Rebels Aren't So Scary." *Wall Street Journal*. February 22, 1995, 5.

U.S. Department of State. *Afghanistan Human Rights Practices, 1994.* Washington D.C.: Government Printing Office, 1994.

Washington Post. Editorial, "A Turn in Afghanistan." February 25, 1995, A16.

Wills, Garry. "The New Revolutionaries." *New York Review of Books.* August 10, 1995, 50–55.

10

Ethics, Chaos, and the Demand for Good Leaders

Joanne Ciulla

Nothing is more essential to leadership and teachership than carefully discerning what to take and what to leave aside. The consummation of taking or leaving is determined within; the beginnings of safety and danger are determined without. (Fushan Yuan in a Letter to Master Jingyin Tai)

The cry for leadership in our society comes in a time of perceived chaos. People want leaders who will provide order; however, the complexity of today's world requires a different kind of leader. Since leaders have limited power to provide order to the external environment, it is crucial that they provide order in human relationships. In a society that is not hierarchical, one way that we supply order is through trust. This is why ethics is and ought to be at the heart of teaching and research in leadership studies. Hence, it is not surprising that all the essays in this collection explicitly or implicitly discuss the ethics of leadership. Paul Johnson's fine essay on Plato and Nietzsche describes two of the fundamental ethical issues in leadership. The first concerns the use of force and persuasion in leadership. The second issue, raised by the Sophists, is the tension between the actions that someone takes to become a leader and the actions of a person once he or she becomes a leader.

Peter Temes's paper on Martin Luther King emphasizes the importance of moral ideas to leadership. He rightly points out that a leader may possess all the right qualities and techniques needed to be a leader, but he or she won't get far if motivated by poor ideals. Leadership, according to Temes, should speak to people's souls. The case of Earl Warren and Thurgood

Marshall and *Brown v. Board of Education* echoes some of the lessons that we learn from Martin Luther King about how moral ideals give leaders power and respect. Mark Sibicky's discussion of the Milgram experiments is about the ethics of obedience and the misuse of authority. The Milgram experiments illustrate a classic ethical problem. When there is pressure to achieve the ends of an action people sometimes use unethical means for achieving their goal. The Milgram experiments also remind us that a leader's words and deeds carry a heavier moral weight and responsibility than the words and deeds of others. Sibicky's essay reminds us that leaders have to be especially reflective about their ethical responsibilities because of their authority over and impact on others. Jacob Heilbrunn also emphasizes the need for more work on the dark side of leadership. How can we understand and guard against the dangerous mixture of paranoia and charisma that constitutes immoral leaders?

In her article on gender, work, and leadership, Judith Lorber raises questions about the way in which one gender has dominated the ethics and values of society and leadership. She leaves the reader wondering if the way women "do leadership" will improve the ethical character of leadership and society. Daniel Born's paper on leadership studies criticizes the idea that communitarians have the answer to the problems of leadership and social morality. While the common good is a part of the ethics of leadership in a democratic society, it is not the whole story.

Ethics hasn't always played a central role in leadership research. Scholars are just beginning to assess the legacy of leadership research, which comes from the social sciences. In their attempt to do value-free social science, researchers of the past filtered out the ethical issues of leadership and in doing so, failed to give us a very good understanding of leadership. This does not mean that the older research is useless, but rather that it only offers small snapshot theories that describe leadership behaviors and traits, but fail to give us a complete picture of leadership. Today most people realize that leadership studies has to be an interdisciplinary field. This means that we need the humanities scholars to do what the social scientists won't do, which is talk about the role of history, art and values in leadership. We also need the social scientists to give us empirical descriptions of behavior.

The ideal state of leadership studies will be one in which people from different disciplines respect each other and learn from each other. I disagree with Born's assertion that leadership studies should become *a* discipline if discipline means that scholars adopt one research methodology or that leadership scholars become jacks-of-all-trades. I would rather see the philosopher incorporating the work of a good psychologist into his or her research, than see the philosopher do mediocre social science and the psychologist do mediocre philosophy. Ideally the philosopher and the social scientist will collaborate on their research. The strength of leadership studies will come from having the best scholars in various disciplines using their various methodologies to investigate leadership. Leadership studies should be the field in which people from different backgrounds work together.

We're at a point in the development of leadership studies where good critical analysis is necessary in order to understand where we have been and where we should be going. Joseph Rost's book *Leadership in the Twenty-First Century* is important because it offers the only well researched book-length critique of the field. Rost's book has invigorated leadership scholars because it offers so many ideas with which to disagree. Like Born and Johnson, I take issue with a number of issues in Rost's book, particularly his ideas about ethics and leadership. However, I also disagree with Rost's contention that the problem with leadership studies is that we lack a common definition. In critiquing Rost's point, I discovered the way in which ethics was embedded in past and present leadership studies.

Ethics and Definitions of Leadership

Leadership scholars have spent time and trouble worrying about the definition of leadership. Rost analyzes 221 definitions to make his point that there is no common definition of leadership. What Rost does not make clear is what he means by a definition. Sometimes he sounds as if a definition supplies necessary and sufficient conditions for identifying leadership. He says, "neither scholars nor the practitioners have been able to define leadership with precision, accuracy, and conciseness so that people are able to label it correctly when they see it happening or when they engage in it" (6). He goes on to say that the various publications and the media all use leadership to mean different things that have little to do with what leadership really is. In places Rost uses the word *definition* as if it were a theory or perhaps a paradigm. He says that a shared definition implies that there is a "school" of leadership. When the definition changes, there is a "paradigm shift" (99).

Rost's claim that what leadership studies needs is a common definition of leadership is off the mark for two reasons. One would be hard-pressed to find a group of sociologists or historians who shared the exact same definition of sociology or history. It is also not clear that the various definitions that Rost examines are that different in terms of what they denote. I selected the following definitions from Rost's book on the basis of what Rost says are definitions most representative of each particular era. We need to look at these definitions and ask the following questions: Are these definitions so different that there is no family resemblance between them, that is, would researchers be talking about different things? Lastly, I will look at what these definitions tell us about the place of ethics in leadership studies.

1920s	[Leadership is] the ability to impress the will of the leader on those led and induce obedience, respect, loyalty and cooperation.
1930s	Leadership is a process in which the activities of many are organized to move in a specific direction by one.
1940s	Leadership is the result of an ability to persuade or direct men, apart from the prestige or power that comes from office or external circumstance.
1950s	[Leadership is what leaders do in groups.] The leader's authority is spontaneously accorded him by his fellow group members.
1960s	[Leadership is] acts by a person which influence other persons in a shared direction.

1970s	Leadership is defined in terms of discretionary influence. Discretionary influence refers to those leader behaviors under the control of the leader which he may vary from individual to individual.
1980s	Regardless of the complexities involved in the study of leadership, its meaning is relatively simple. Leadership means to inspire others to undertake some form of purposeful action as determined by the leader.
1990s	Leadership is an influence relationship between leaders and followers who intend real changes that reflect their mutual purposes. (Rost offers a range of sources for these and other related definitions of leadership; see his pages 47, 48, 50, 53, 72, 102).

If we look at the sample of definitions from different periods, we see that the problem of definition is not that scholars have radically different denotations of leadership. One can detect a family resemblance between the different definitions. All of them talk about leadership as some kind of process, act, or influence that in some way gets people to do something. A roomful of people, each holding one of these definitions, would understand each other.

Where the definitions differ is in their connotation, particularly in terms of their implications for the leader/follower relationship. In other words, *how* leaders get people to do things (impress, organize, persuade, influence, and inspire) and *how* what is to be done is decided (obedience, voluntary consent, determined by the leader, and reflection of mutual purposes) have normative implications. So perhaps what Rost is really talking about is not definitions, but theories about how people lead (or how people *should* lead) and the relationship of leaders to those who are led. His critique of particular definitions is really a critique of the way they do or don't describe the underlying moral commitments of the leader/follower relationship.

If the above definitions imply that leadership is some sort of relationship between leaders and followers in which something happens or gets done, then the next question is, How do we describe this relationship? For people who believe in the values of a democratic society such as freedom and equality, the most morally unattractive definitions are those that appear to be coercive, manipulative and disregard the input of followers. Rost clearly dislikes the theories from the 1920s, 1970s and 1980s, not because they are inaccurate, but because he rejects the authoritarian values inherent in them. Nonetheless, theories such as the ones from the 1920s, 1970s and 1980s, may be quite accurate if we observed the way some corporate and world leaders behave.

The most morally attractive definitions hail from the 1940s, 1950s, 1960s and Rost's own definition of the 1990s. They imply a non-coercive participatory and democratic relationship between leaders and followers. There are two morally appealing elements of these theories. First, rather than *induce*, these leaders *influence*, which implies that leaders recognize the autonomy of followers. Rost's definition uses the word influence, which carries an implication that there is some degree of voluntary compliance on the part of followers. In Rost's chapter on ethics he says, "The leadership process is ethical if the people in the relationship (the leaders and followers) *freely* agree that the intended changes fairly reflect their mutual purposes" (161). For Rost consensus is an important part of what makes leadership *leadership* and it does so because free choice is morally pleasing to most people. The second morally attractive part of these definitions is they imply recognition of the beliefs, values, and needs of the followers. Followers are the leader's partner in shaping the goals and purposes of a group or organization.

Good Leadership and Effective Leadership

The morally attractive definitions also speak to a distinction frequently made between leadership and headship (or positional leadership). Holding a formal leadership position or position of power does not necessarily mean that a person exercises leadership. Furthermore, you do not have to hold a formal position in order to exercise leadership. Leaders can wield force or authority using only their position and the resources and power that come with it. This is an important distinction, but it does not get us out of "the Hitler problem."

The Hitler problem is, How do you answer the question, "Is Hitler a leader?" Under the morally unattractive definitions he is a leader, perhaps even a great leader, albeit an immoral one. Ron Heifitz argues that under the great man and trait theories of leadership you can put Hitler, Lincoln and Gandhi in the same category because the underlying value of the theory is that leadership is influence over history (28). However, under the morally attractive theories, Hitler is not a leader at all. He's a bully or tyrant or simply the head of Germany.

To muddy the waters even further, according to one of Warren Bennis's and Burt Nanus's characterizations of leadership, "The manager does things right and the leader does the right thing," one could argue that Hitler is neither unethical nor a leader, he is a manager (45). Bennis and Nanus are among those management writers who talk as if all leaders are wonderful and all managers morally flabby drones. However, what appears to be behind this in Bennis's and Nanus's work is the idea that leaders *are* or *should be* morally a head above everyone else.

So what does this all mean? It looks like we are back to the problem of definition again. The first and obvious meaning is that definitions of leadership have normative implications. Leadership scholars such as Bennis and Nanus are sloppy about the language they use to describe and prescribe. While it is true that researchers have to be clear about when they are describing and when they are prescribing, the crisp fact/value distinction will not in itself improve our understanding of leadership.

Leadership scholars who worry about constructing the ultimate definition of leadership are asking the wrong question, but inadvertently trying to answer the right question. As we have seen from the examination of definitions, the ultimate question in leadership studies is not "What *is* the definition of leadership?" The ultimate point of studying leadership is, "What is *good* leadership?" The use of the word *good* here has two senses, morally good and technically good or effective. These two senses form a logical conjunction. In other words, in order for the statement "She is a good leader" to be true, it must be true that she is effective and she is ethical. The question of what constitutes a good leader lies at the heart of the public debate on leadership. We want our leaders to be good in both ways. It's easy to judge if they are effective, but more difficult to judge if they are ethical because there is some confusion over what factors are relevant to making this kind of assessment.

The problem with the existing leadership research is that few studies investigate both senses of good and when they do, they usually do not fully explore the moral implications of their research questions or their results. The research on leadership effectiveness touches indirectly on the problem of explicitly articulating the normative implications of descriptive research. The Ohio Studies and the Michigan Studies both measured leadership effectiveness in terms of how leaders treated subordinates and how they got the job done. The Ohio Studies measured leadership effectiveness in terms of consideration, the degree to which leaders act in a friendly and supportive manner, and initiating structure, or the way that leaders structure their own role and the role of subordinates in order to obtain group goals (Fleishman, 1–6). The Michigan Studies measured leaders on the basis of task orientation and relationship orientation (see Leikert's two volumes). These two studies spawned a number of other research programs and theories, including the situational leadership theory of Hershey and Blanchard, which looks at effectiveness in terms of how leaders adapt their leadership style to the requirements of a situation. Some situations require a task orientation, others a relationship orientation.

Implicit in all of these theories and research programs is an ethical question: Are leaders more effective when they are nice to people, or are leaders more effective when they use certain techniques for structuring and ordering tasks? One would hope that the answer is both, but that answer is not conclusive in the studies that have taken place over the last three decades. The interesting question is, "What if this sort of research shows that you don't have to be kind and considerate to other people to run a country or a profitable organization?" Would scholars and practitioners draw an *ought* from the *is* of this research? It's hard to tell when researchers are not explicit about their ethical commitments. The point is that no matter how much empirical information we get from the "scientific" study of leadership, it will always be inadequate if we neglect the moral implications. It is also true that moral theories on leadership will not be very useful if they ignore the empirical research. Teaching and research in leadership studies requires us to respect the input of other disciplines. Nonetheless, all leadership scholars and teachers are really interested in is good and bad leadership

The Cry for Leadership

Both Born and Heilbrunn refer to John Gardner's "leadership vaccine." Gardner argues that life in a complex society inoculates people against leadership. Barbara Kellerman continues this lament by pointing out that our society has developed an anti-leadership culture that denigrates anyone who wants to become a leader. One offshoot of both remarks is that because of these factors, we either don't get enough leaders or the ones that we get aren't the best ones that we could have. I agree with Gardner and Kellerman, but I think that there is more about the context in which we lie that has led to the felt need for leadership programs and courses.

There is a sense in many Western democracies that leaders are weak and the sources of authority and values are no longer clear. On the news we see a world plagued with crime, terrorism, genocide, and civil wars that are incomprehensible and have no end in sight. The world benefits from the watchful eye of the media that unmasks the atrocities of tyrants, but the media have also made heroes impossible. Few people lead lives so morally perfect that they can stand up to the scrutiny of the press. (For example, I was distressed to learn that there is even an unflattering documentary on Mother Teresa.) In America this problem with the press has gotten so bad that I'm beginning to think that the only people who can be president are people who never engaged in sex, politics, or business.

We live in chaotic times. In ancient Greek, chaos meant an empty space or an abyss. If there is an abyss today it's the sense people have of a void in society because there doesn't seem to be a shared set of ethical values. Scientists describe chaos as the dynamic relationships of phenomena. A small change in initial conditions can have a large effect in the outcome. The "butterfly effect" notes how the flapping of a butterfly's wings in the Amazon can affect the weather in New York. For example, consider how the actions of a Mexican guerrilla leader lowered the value of the peso, which in turn put the American dollar into a free fall, and made it more expensive to buy German and Japanese cars and appliances.

We ordinarily use the word chaos to mean confusion, but as we see from the butterfly effect, chaos doesn't mean that events are causally disconnected. The mystery of chaos is that a small change at one point in time in one location can have a large effect later. Even when events are connected in a predictable way you can get unpredictable results. So, in this chaotic world, what does it take to be an effective leader? One role of leaders is to supply people with things they need. Our society seems to lack order, certainty, and a sense of continuity and control over the future. No leader has control over the external forces of politics, economics, or business, nor is it wise in a chaotic world to run an organization as a monolith. As Heilbrunn points out, in complex institutions such as government it is wrong to think that leadership will provide a quick fix because other factors, such as institutions, shape the problems and policies of the country. If people today want leaders who can control chaos, then they are bound to be disappointed. This is one reason why there is wide dissatisfaction with leaders in every segment of American life. Our disillusionment with leaders is not just a problem with leaders, but a problem with followers. Leaders aren't able to control as much as they used to, which means that followers have to control more. Our chaotic world requires a new kind of leader and follower. Yet many people still cling to the desire for an all powerful and wise leader who will show them the way. The problems of people living and working together are problems that reoccur at different times and in different forms. We can always learn from history.

How Plato Learned About Leadership

Johnson and a number of other leadership scholars have their students read Plato's *Republic*. In the *Republic*, the ideal leaders are philosopher-kings who are wise and benevolent. They rule over a stratified society where everyone has a place based on his or her abilities. While there is much to commend the philosopher-king, it is hard to imagine him being very effective. It takes more than wisdom of universal forms to lead.

What is most interesting about reading Plato is learning how his ideas about leadership evolved. Plato learned about leadership from his three disastrous trips to Syracuse. The first time he was invited by the tyrant Dionysius I. Plato was disgusted by the decadent and luxurious lifestyle of Dionysius' court. He returned to Athens convinced that existing forms of government were corrupt and unstable. Plato then decided to set up the Academy, where he taught for 40 years. It was also at this time that he wrote the *Republic*.

In the *Republic*, Plato argued that the perfect state could only come about by rationally exploiting the highest qualities in people. Such a state would be led by a philosopher-king. Plato firmly believed that the philosopher-king could be developed through education. About 24 years after his first visit, Plato was invited back to Syracuse by Dion, who was Dionysius' brother-in-law. By this time Dionysius I was dead. Dion read the *Republic* and wanted Plato to come and test his theory of leadership education on Dionysius' very promising son Dionysius II. This was an offer that Plato couldn't refuse, although he had serious reservations about accepting it. Anyway, the trip was a disaster. Plato's friend Dion was exiled because of court intrigues. Plato left Syracuse in a hurry, despite young Dionysius' pleas for him to stay.

Upon returning to Athens, Plato wrote,

> the more I advance in years, the harder it appeared to me to administer government correctly. For one thing, nothing could be done without loyal friends and loyal companions, since our city was no longer administered according to the standards and practices of our fathers. Furthermore the written laws and the customs were being corrupted at an astounding rate. The result was that I, who had first been full of eagerness for a public career, as I gazed upon the whirlpool of public life and saw the incessant movement of shifting currents, at last felt dizzy.... (Letters VII, 325c–326; Hamilton 1575)

Plato too saw his world as a chaotic place. Nonetheless he was lured back to Syracuse a third time because Dionysius II promised to make amends with Dion and allow him back into the country. Instead, Dionysius sold all of Dion's property and put Plato under house arrest. Needless to say, when Plato got home from that visit he changed his view of leadership. He lost faith in his conviction that people could be perfected. Leaders shared the same human weaknesses of their followers.

In the *Republic* Plato entertained a pastoral image of the leader as a shepherd to his flock. But in a later work, *The Statesman*, he says that a leader is not at all like a shepherd. Shepherds are obviously quite different from their flock, whereas human leaders are not much different from their followers (*Plato 1992*, 275b–c). Furthermore, people are not sheep, some are cooperative and some are very stubborn. Hence, Plato's revised view was that leaders are really like weavers. Their main task is to weave together into a society different kinds of people such as the meek and self-controlled and the brave and impetuous (310e).

If we follow the progression of Plato's work on leadership, he goes from a profound belief that it is possible for some people to be wise and benevolent philosopher-kings, to a more modest belief that the real challenge of leadership is getting people who sometimes don't like each other, don't like the leader, and don't want to work together, to work toward a common goal. Jim O'Toole says that leadership is more like being a shepherd to a flock of cats than a flock of sheep (6). Sometimes leadership is like pushing a cart full of frogs.

As Johnson points out, the *Republic* gets at some of the pivotal issues in leadership such as justice and the importance of a universal notion of good. Near the end of the *Statesman* Plato contends that we can't always depend on leaders to be good and that is why we need rule of law (300c–d). For example in the case of Earl Warren and Thurgood Marshall, we not only see exemplars of sound leadership in the Supreme Court, but we see decisions of issues such as desegregation that make the law do what we cannot always depend on leaders to do. Good laws serve as leadership substitutes and help us to survive poor leadership. It would be interesting to see research on the relationship between confidence in our nation's leadership and the desire to tinker with the Constitution. For example, Does the proposal for a balanced budget amendment to the Constitution reflect a belief that we cannot trust leaders to balance the budget?

The Jepson School

In America people are disappointed by both leadership *and* the law and like Plato, their reaction is to try and educate people to do a better job. Today we are not only frustrated by ineffective leaders, but by immoral ones. As I have pointed out earlier the two issues are intertwined. The disillusionment with leadership has led to the development of leadership programs in high schools, universities, business, and government.

The Jepson School of Leadership Studies is the first school of leadership in the country to offer a bachelor's degree in leadership studies. It was started with a 20 million dollar donation by University of Richmond alumnus Bob Jepson. I was one of the four faculty members and two deans who designed the Jepson School curriculum. From the beginning, we realized that the charge of our school went beyond management courses or skills courses. We were also very clear about the fact that this program would not follow the model of leadership programs in military schools, despite the fact that the first Dean of the school came from West Point.

The purpose of the school was "to educate people for and about leadership." Our mission was "to prepare students to take on the moral responsibilities of leadership." We envisioned all leadership, whether in business, government, communities, or social movements, as service to society. None of us saw the school as an exclusive training ground for future presidents and CEO's. Like Heilbrunn we did not think that everyone could be educated to be a great leader. Students take courses in art, history, and physics, but we don't assume they will all be great artists, historians, or physicists and the same is true of leadership studies. We had a broader vision of the school as a place where we developed citizens and people who would be capable of taking on formal and informal leadership roles in a business, a community, or a citizens group.

Our educational goals coincide with the classical definition of the liberal arts. The liberal arts were those arts that teach people how to live in a free society. In order to educate leaders for a chaotic world, we would need all of the liberal arts, from history and literature to science and psychology. In a chaotic world one of the most important abilities of a leader is to correctly understand current conditions, because as chaos scientists tell us, even with causally determinate systems, any small error in sizing up the initial conditions will lead to unexpected results. In this respect leadership entails mastery of the fine art of sensing the whole or, as Temes points out, leadership students need to understand society.

The Jepson School is still a work in progress. The core courses in the two-year program are History and Theories of Leaders, Critical Thinking, Leading Groups, and Ethics and Leadership. In the limited assessment feedback that we have from the first graduating class, it is interesting to note that of the four courses, students tend to find Critical Thinking most helpful in the outside world, and the history and theories of leadership course least helpful. However, within the history and theories course, they tend to like the history part best. The sample is too small to draw any conclusions yet, but the students' attitudes regarding the usefulness of traditional leadership theory may speak to the one-dimensional nature of the old theories that come out of psychology and business research. The other elements of the Jepson School leadership program are a list of competency courses such as conflict resolution, decision making, policy making. Students are also required to study leadership in two different contexts. So far students can choose from four context courses: political leadership, community leadership, social movement leadership and leadership in formal organizations such as business and government. We are rethinking, changing, and expanding this category. For example, it would be useful to have a course on leadership in an international context.

Service learning is also a required part of the Jepson School program, but it does not derive from communitarian ideals that Born describes in his article. We place our students in a variety of community service agencies for a semester and then students meet in a seminar to discuss their experiences. I was skeptical about service learning at first because I was uncomfortable with the idea of *forced* service. However, after teaching the seminar, I discovered that service learning played an important role in the development of our students. Service learning gives students an opportunity to take on leadership roles with people who are very different from themselves. The young woman who was given charge of an after-school program for inner city teenagers learned that they were not happy to see her and they did not appreciate her "help," and didn't respect her despite her role. She learned about class difference and that respect must be earned. Two football players who worked on a children's playground discovered that the 7-year-olds wouldn't obey them. They too reflected on the way in which a leader gains respect and authority. Students got to think about who they were and their place in regard to others in the socioeconomic strata of society. They gained perspective, confidence and humility from their experience. Most important, service learning helps students appreciate how difficult it is to lead. It is education that tends to hit them more in the heart than in the head, but it's also the kind of educational experience that should not be left to chance. Service learning demands careful planning and facilitation by the instructor.

Ethics, Chaos, and Power

Earlier I said that in times of chaos people expect leaders to provide some certainty and order to their worlds. In a chaotic environment a leader doesn't have perfect control. While leaders cannot offer control over the external environment that affects a company or a society, they can fill the need of followers for stability by being trustworthy. Trust allows people to feel that there is order in their relationship with others. This is why there is so much concern over the ethics of leaders in all walks of life.

Ethics is central to leadership in a chaotic world. Those who doubt the importance of ethics point to highly effective but unethical leaders of the past and argue that ethics didn't seem relevant to their ability to get the job done. That state of affairs no longer exists. In liberal societies force as a source of power and control is generally considered illegitimate, and so is physical exploitation of people. In a chaotic world, there are so many related variables that are affected by so many people that it is difficult to force people to act by the stick or by the carrot. Unlike unethical but effective leaders of the past, it is very hard to keep evil ways secret for long in a society that has an active press, efficient communication systems, and sensible regulations. Sophisticated global telecommunications make it hard for repressive regimes to keep a lid on their dirty secrets. A strong set of ethical values is an inherently powerful motivator that provides the stability that people need to keep adapting to change.

Our high-tech world has gotten more personal. Access to information makes us feel that we know our leaders better, and because we know them better, we are more concerned about their personal ethics. Information is also power and information technology equalizes the power of leaders and subordinates. In the past only the leaders of powerful nations held the tools of destruction, today anyone can become a terrorist. Power has become fragmented and good and evil particularized.

In order to develop the kind of leaders that we need to be effective in a chaotic world, we have to change the way we think about power. Most organizations use power as a reward. If you do a good job, you move up into a position where you have more power over other people and other people have less power over you. Governments and organizations in the United States and other parts of the world have been on a crash diet. They realize that they have to cut costs and learn to do more with less people. The flattening of organizations and the removal of layers of middle managers have made it necessary to give more responsibility to people lower down in organizations. This is one reason why business and government organizations run leadership programs.

It is very difficult for people in leadership roles to give up power. According to Lorber, leadership in these flattened organizations requires leaders who are accessible and grant autonomy, while at the same time demanding that subordinates perform well. Some authors argue that women possess the qualities needed for this new kind of leadership. However, Lorber points out that the reason women tend to be better at this kind of leadership is because they are usually in weaker leadership positions and need the help and good will of subordinates, without having the power and resources to offer them material rewards.

Nowadays, leaders at all levels seem to be in this position. Leaders can still use the stick on subordinates, but they have fewer carrots to hand out. They also really need the help of others, because of the complex chaotic environment in which all organizations operate. Leaders have to know how to build good will and consensus. Leadership teachers and scholars also should pay more attention to the role of conflict in leadership. These are necessities because of the changing nature of power. The paradox of consensus is that we like the idea of consensus, but consensus does not always yield the best solutions to problems. Rost fails to understand this point. Sometimes a moral leader has to go against the wishes of his or her constituents in order to do what is morally right.

Personal Morality

An inherent part of the ethics of leadership is the way in which a person gets power and the kind of power he or she wields. Leadership educators have to help students understand the moral hazards of power. In every election we try to size up the ethics of the candidates. Ethics is also a favored tool of political assassination in politics. The most common way of predicting whether someone will be an ethical leader is by looking at his or her past. This is a very complicated process because we have to first pick out what is important and then project that into future behavior. We usually choose what is most important by what is most interesting. This is determined by a kind of telepathy between mass media and the public. Sex is usually what is most interesting, even if it isn't what is most relevant.

The time frame matters when we make judgments on leaders. What we know now about a candidate's past matters because we try to use that information as a predictor of future success as a leader. History loves a winner and reflects the human inclination for forgiveness. James MacGregor Burns tells us about the successes of Roosevelt, but he also lets us know about some of Roosevelt's dirty tricks. When we weigh the pluses and minuses in our own minds and consider that it is all in the past, we are willing to forget the bad and remember the good. We now know that Martin Luther King Jr. and John F. Kennedy were womanizers. It doesn't seem to matter much looking back. But we don't know whether these scandals would have affected their leadership when they were alive.

When students look at case studies and historical accounts of leaders they need to appreciate the fact that the most ethical leaders in history are often the ones with the most amount of moral luck. Some luck is extrinsic and some luck is intrinsic. You need both for success. Intrinsic moral luck is related to intentions and estimates about your ability to succeed at some task. Extrinsic moral luck consists of factors that you cannot control (Williams, 26). When faced with difficult ethical problems, we are usually faced with uncertainty of outcome. People can have good intentions—know what the right thing is and why they should do it, but also know that things may not turn out all right. Almost all revered military heroes had moral luck. There are only a few who for the right reasons stormed the hill, did no damage to the enemy, and had all of their men slaughtered. Think how one event in history could have changed our view of a leader. What would have happened to Jimmy Carter if the helicopters hadn't broken down during the military mission to rescue the hostages in Iran? Carter had rotten moral luck.

Philosophers have long debated how you judge the morality of people. John Stuart Mill said that the end of a person's act tells you about the morality of the act. The intentions and the means of doing the act tell you about the morality of the person. This sensible view of morality is very problematic when it comes to leadership. The public debate over the ethics of leaders is sometimes unable to sort this out because of an overemphasis on leaders as role models. We have a strong need for moral leaders that we can trust and we want leaders with a track record of doing good things. It is difficult to sort out who is morally good but unlucky, and who is morally shaky, but lucky. The press recognized this problem when they labeled Reagan the "Teflon President."

The moral foible that the public fears most in a leader is personal immorality accompanied by an abuse of power. Dean Ludwig and Clinton Longenecker call this abuse the Bathsheba Syndrome. In the story of David and Bathsheba we learn how

David came home from the front and while walking around his palace, he happened to see Bathsheba bathing. He seduces Bathsheba and she gets pregnant. King David tries to cover it up by calling her husband home from the front and getting him drunk so that he will sleep with Bathsheba. Her husband won't cooperate because he feels it would be unfair to enjoy himself while his men are still in danger.

The Bathsheba story demonstrates our worst fears about the private morality of leaders in office. First, we fear that successful leaders will loose strategic focus—David should have been thinking about the war, not watching Bathsheba bathe. This is why we worry about womanizers getting distracted from their jobs. Second, power leads to privileged access. Leaders have more opportunities to indulge themselves. David can just have Bathsheba brought to him by his servants, no questions asked. And third, powerful leaders have control over resources, which sometimes gives them an inflated belief in their ability to control outcomes. David gets involved in escalating cover-ups. In the end, he pays dearly for his actions.

The interesting thing about the Bathsheba syndrome is that it is hard to predict because people get it after they have become successful. It is a reaction to the temptations of power. Someone may be perfectly ethical in his or her past professional life and then change. Leaders of respected organizations like the United Way and the NAACP were committed activists for their cause, but lost their focus and misused their organizations' money and resources once they obtained leadership positions. Nixon misused his office to cover-up the Watergate break-in. We need to tell these stories to our students. Power is one of the most ethically difficult parts of leadership and life in general.

Our chaotic complex world requires leadership at all levels of organizations and society. Technology, the mass media, and the free market give everyone more power by providing access to information and resources. This power needs to be used responsibly. The distance between leaders and followers has narrowed. Leadership programs have not emerged to produce "great men" or "great women," they have emerged to produce responsible citizens, who have an understanding of the world they live in and possess the will and ability to take on leadership roles.

The future of leadership studies depends on the quality of its scholars and the commitment of its teachers. With the entry of scholars from different disciplines the field is going through a renaissance. The field will continue to evolve with experience, research, and social change. We will take on new ideas and leave aside old ones. However, the one thing I hope we never again leave aside is the role of ethics in the study and teaching of leadership.

Works Cited

Fleishman, E.A. "The Description of Supervisory Behavior." *Personnel Journal* 37 (1963): 1–6.

Leikert, R. *New Patterns of Management*. New York: McGraw-Hill, 1961.

———. *The Human Organization: Its Management and Value*. New York: McGraw-Hill, 1967.

O'Toole, James. *Leading Change*. San Francisco: Jossey-Bass, 1995.

Plato. *The Statesman*. Tr. J. B. Skemp. Indianapolis, IN: Hacket Publishing, 1992.

———. *Collected Dialogues*. Ed. Edith Hamilton and Huntington Cairns. Princeton: Princeton University Press, 1971.

Williams, Bernard. *Moral Luck*. New York:Cambridge University Press, 1981.

Wittgenstein, Ludwig. *Philosophical Investigations*. 3e. Tr. G.E.M. Anscomb. New York: Macmillan, 1968.